D1465783

FIELD SPORTS LIBRARY

FALCONRY
IN
THE
BRITISH ISLES

NOTE ON CONTENT

Because the art of Falconry has changed little since the book was first written the reader will find much of value in these pages. However, some of the figures on costs are obviously out of date and some modern falconers might say that some of the methods used have now been improved upon.

More importantly is the fact that birds in the British Isles are protected by various acts and keeping birds of prey will require a licence. The *Wildlife & Countryside Act, 1981* and its subsequent amendments have given much more protection to birds and readers are advised to study the appropriate legislation for guidance. A useful magazine for information is *Cage & Aviary Birds*.

FALCONRY
IN
THE
BRITISH ISLES

Francis Henry Salvin
William Brodrick

Beech Publishing House
Station Yard
Elsted
Midhurst
West Sussex, GU29 0JT

ISBN 1-85736-094-X

First published in 1855 with a second edition in 1873, a modern re-issue was made in 1972.

British Library Cataloguing-in-Publication Data
A catalogue record for this this book is available from the British Library.

Beech Publishing House
Station Yard
Elsted
Midhurst
West Sussex, GU29 0JT

Printed and bound in Malta by Interprint Limited.

CONTENTS

LIST OF PLATES
Painted by William Brodrick
These appear after page vii.

Plate I.

FEMALE PEREGRINE (young)

Plate II.

MALE PEREGRINE (1 year old)

Plate III.

MALE PEREGRINE (adult)

Plate IV.

(Female) PEREGRINE (adult)
(dark variety)

Plate V.

MALE PEREGRINE ON THE CADGE (adult)

Plate VI.

FEMALE ICELAND FALCON (adult)
(dark variety)

Plate VII.

MALE MERLINS (adult and young)

Plate VIII.

FEMALE MERLIN (young)

Plate IX.

HOBBIES (adult male and young female)

Plate X.

(Male) ICELAND FALCON (adult)
(light variety)

Plate XI.

MALE ICELAND FALCON (young)

Plate XII.

(Male) GREENLAND FALCON (adult)

Plate XIII.

FEMALE GREENLAND FALCON (young)

Plate XIV.

(Male) NORWAY FALCON (2nd year)

Plate XV.

SAKER (adult female)

Plate XVI.

LANNER

Plate XVII.

BARBARY FALCON (young male)

Plate XVIII.

MALE GOSHAWK (adult)

Plate XIX.

FEMALE GOSHAWK (young)

Plate XX.

MALE SPARROW HAWK (adult)

Plate XXI.

FEMALE SPARROW HAWK (young)

Plate XXII.

IMPLEMENTS

Plate XXIII.

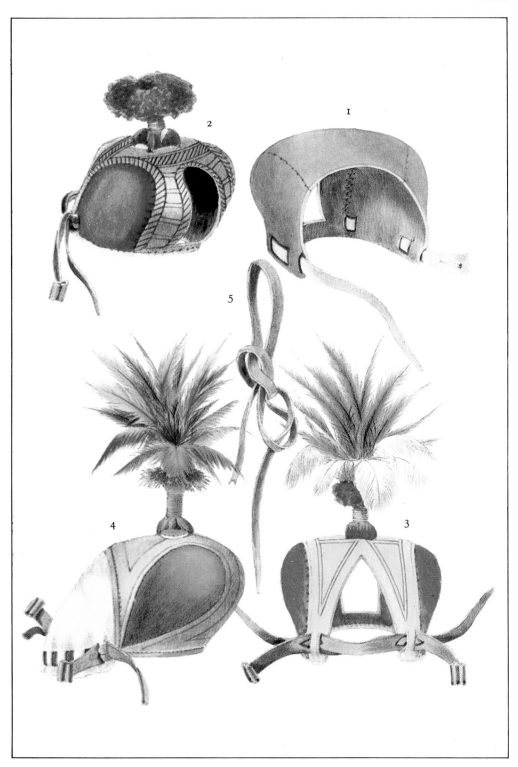

IMPLEMENTS

Plate XXIV.

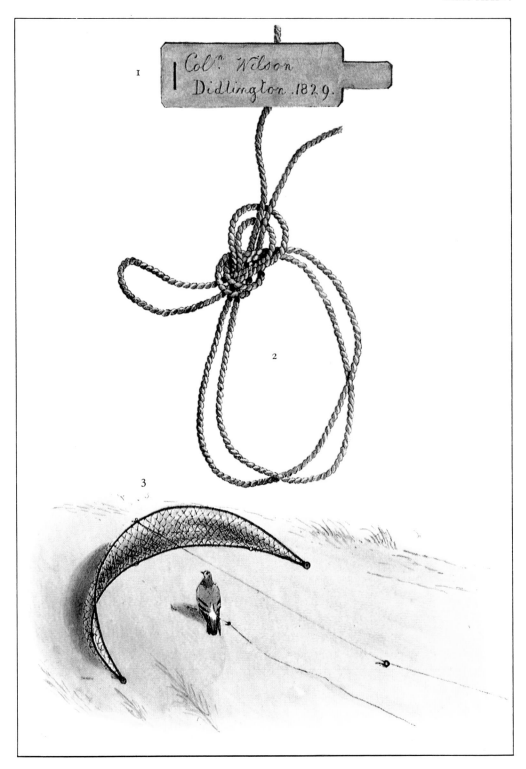

IMPLEMENTS

FALCONRY

IN

THE BRITISH ISLES.

INTRODUCTION.

So little at the present day is practically known on the subject of Falconry, that the Authors of the following work have been induced to put together the result of some few years' personal experience in the art, with the hope of inducing others to take up a sport from which they themselves have derived so much pleasure, and at the same time of aiding the young beginner in so doing. In this attempt they have been greatly assisted by the valuable contributions of other Falconers and friends, all of which they gratefully acknowledge. Sir John Sebright's 'Observations on Hawking' gives the sketch from which they hope to fill up the picture; and in this endeavour it will be their aim to carry with them the young Falconer, the general Sportsman, as well as the Naturalist, from whom they must crave indulgence for the numerous defects, of which their very slight acquaintance with the

"Art of Writing" is at once the cause, and must be the apology.

The Figures of the Birds are in all cases where practicable taken from life, and are in several instances faithful portraits of living trained birds; they are drawn to scale, one-third of the natural proportions.

To commence with the early history of Falconry, but little is known concerning its origin; probably the East was the birth-place, as it remains to this day the stronghold, of the art. We are informed by Mr. Layard, in the second volume of his interesting work on Nineveh and Babylon, that, upon his visiting the ruins of Khorsabad, he found a bas-relief, " in which there appeared to be a Falconer bearing a hawk on his wrist; " and although the hand of Time has weighed heavily upon this record of the past, in all probability so accurate an observer was not mistaken in his surmise. Perhaps as old as this carving is a curious seal from Syria, in the collection of W. B. Barker, Esq., the author of ' Cilicia and its Governors.' This valuable antique evidently represents a Dog and Hawk in pursuit of a Hare. The only trace we can discover of the art as having been practised at an early period in Europe, is from a passage in Pliny, in which he speaks of a particular part of Thrace where "men and hawks were used to hunt their prey together; the men beating the woods, and the hawks pouncing on the birds they disturbed." As, however, this author does not make any mention of the practice, or mode of training Hawks, it is impossible to believe that it was an art ever known to the Romans, at any rate not until quite the latter period of the Empire. It might have reached them, as it probably did this, and the neighbouring countries, borne on a wave of that mighty human tide, which, receiving its first impulse in the extreme north-eastern tracts

of Asia, swept during the fifth century over the continent of
Europe. In England, Falconry cannot be traced beyond the
reign of Ethelbert, A.D. 860 (as Pennant tells us). From
that time, however, until the middle of the seventeenth century* it was the favourite amusement of all, from the monarch to the page; and one in which the fair sex took particular delight. To such an extent was it patronized, that,
during several reigns very stringent laws were passed for the
better protection of the various species of Hawks made use of;
certain species being at the same time allotted to particular
ranks and orders of men, the highest being alone privileged
to carry the most noble birds.

We find representations of this sport upon the most
ancient Tapestry, as the Bayeux Tapestry worked by Matilda
of Flanders, Queen of William the Conqueror, where Harrold
is seen approaching the Duke of Normandy with a hawk
upon his wrist.

We have also some fine examples of it in several manu-
scripts, as for example the 'Louterell Psalter,' time of
Edward II., in the possession of Joseph Weld, Esq. of Lul-
worth Castle.

In the fifth volume of the New Series of the 'Art Journal,'
p. 170, will be found some interesting remarks upon Hawking, under the title of "The Domestic Manners of the English
during the Middle Ages," by Thomas Wright, Esq., F.S.A.
Indeed this subject at one time engrossed so much attention,
that few works were altogether silent upon it; hence 'The
Paston Letters' and most old Diaries mention it as a favourite
amusement.

Falconry took a prominent part in Heraldry, of which the

---

* As we meet with no new enactments with respect to Hawking or the Game
Laws during the Commonwealth, and as we know that sports in general were not
countenanced by the Covenanters, we infer that Falconry received so severe a
check during Cromwell's time, that it did not recover its ground for upwards of
a century, viz. until somewhere about 1770 or 1780, as we shall hereafter show.

examples are so numerous that we need only select one, viz.
the badge of Edward IV. for the Dukedom of York. This
was a Falcon and Fetterlock—a Falcon displayed *argent*
within a closed fetterlock *Or**. This may be seen on the
brass gates of Henry VII.'s Chapel at Westminster.

We are indebted to Mr. Barker (mentioned at page 2) for
much valuable information with respect to the training and
management of the Goshawk, and on the Assyrian mode of
using Hawks in general; and on comparing this mode with
the European system of Falconry, it will be found that a great
similarity exists between the two. From the many ingenious
contrivances which we have in common with the Eastern
Falconers, we conclude that both nations have derived their
art from one original system, which has varied but little with
the lapse of ages, and which the intercourse between the East
and West at the time of the Crusades may have tended to
strengthen. There can be no doubt that, at a later period,
upon the continent, Napoleon's wars broke up Falconry. In
this country, at least in Scotland, it has always retained its
admirers; these, however, have been so limited in number,
from the time of the civil wars, that by many it has been
supposed that at one period there were not any native Falconers by profession remaining. Sir John Sebright tells us
that all the Falconers he had met with, either in England or
on the continent, came from Valkenswaard, a village near to
Bois le Duc in Holland: this village has been from time immemorial, and is even to this day, famous for its Falconers,
but we cannot go so far as to pronounce its inhabitants the
only European Falconers. About the close of the eighteenth
century, Lord Orford† and Colonel Thornton made a considerable effort to revive Hawking in this country, for which end
they introduced the "Dutch school of Falconry" into

---

* This monarch granted this badge to an ancestor of the present Sir Henry
Bedingfield, Bart.

† The third Earl, and uncle to Horace Walpole.

England; but this (the Dutch system of Hawking*) never extended into Scotland, which always had its own native Falconers. Of the Valkenswaard Falconers, who from time to time came to England, we may name John Daims, who was in Lord Orford's service; John Bekkers, and his two sons Peter and John; Peter and Lambert Dankers; Peter Koppen; Peter Weymans, and Francis Van den Heurel were with Colonel Thornton; James Bots was with Major Wilson†; John Pells‡ divided his services for many years between several gentlemen. These Falconers probably assisted in reviving a taste for this ancient sport in England, and they also might have imparted much information respecting the catching of Wild Hawks and the treatment of these birds, as also the training necessary and the management in the field of some flights, to which we were strangers, such as Kite, Hare, and Heron Hawking upon " the *passage*." At the same time

* This chiefly differed from the Scotch school in the Dutch using " Passage Hawks," whereas the Scotch used " Eyesses."

† Major Wilson (afterwards Colonel Wilson) became Lord Berners; and here we may remark, that he was of the same family as the famous Dame Juliana Berners, Abbess of Sopwell near St. Albans, who wrote upon Falconry about the year 1460.

‡ This excellent Falconer was born at Valkenswaard, about A.D. 1778. When a boy of eleven he went to assist the Falconers of the Landgrave of Hesse Cassel, who was then the greatest Falconer upon the continent. There were always some Jer Falcons in this establishment, and it was there that Pells made himself so well acquainted with the nature and treatment of this noble Falcon. Pells came to England about 1800, and for many years he was principally with John Hall, Esq., of Weston Colville, Cambridgeshire, during the game season, and with Colonel Wilson in the spring for the Heron Hawking. He was also in the service of J. Downes, Esq., of Old Gunton Hall, Suffolk. Afterwards he was engaged by the Duke of Leeds, and in 1832 by the Duke of St. Albans. He died in 1838, and was succeeded by his son John, who is at present the Duke of St. Albans' Falconer. His Grace the Duke of Leeds has an oil painting by Giles of Aberdeen, in which Pells is represented feeding the Duke's favourite Tiercel " the General."

Napoleon the First presented this Falconer with a rich Falconer's bag, which is now in the possession of the Duke of Leeds.

they learnt from us the mode of using Eyesses, to which, in their country*, they could not have been accustomed. In proof, however, that we do not owe our present knowledge on the subject exclusively to this " *Dutch school of Falconry*," and that the art had never been without its native professors in this kingdom, we have but to recollect that *we alone* used varvels upon our Hawks' jesses, which the Dutch never used. These varvels were rings of silver, upon which was engraved the owner's address, and are thus written evidences of our previous knowledge of Falconry. Varvels were used until these foreigners introduced their method of fastening Hawks with a swivel and longer jesses, which was afterwards generally adopted. As a further proof, we may select a few Scotch-bred Falconers who learnt Falconry entirely from native predecessors.

The most remarkable instance of a succession of Falconers from father to son for many generations occurs in the ancient family of the Flemings of Barochan Tower, Renfrewshire. The present possessor kept Hawks in India, his father kept the Renfrewshire subscription Hawks† until his death in

---

* The coast of Holland as well as the interior of the country being flat, and without rocks, is not suitable to the nidification of the Peregrine, hence the Dutch knew but little of Eyesses, but were excellent Falconers with *Passage Hawks*. They have for ages taken the Peregrine on its passage during the autumn migration over the extensive flats of their country. In the spring they train and enter these Hawks at Herons.

† There is a very interesting picture at Barochan, painted about 1811 by Howe, which represents this Mr. Fleming, his Falconer (the famous John Anderson), and George Harvey, an assistant; the horse, dogs, &c. were all excellent portraits. There is an engraving of this oil painting published by Messrs. Finley of Glasgow. There is also a picture at Barochan of John Anderson. It is a faithful likeness of him as he appeared in a court-dress (of the time of James the First) on the 19th of July, 1821, at the coronation of George the Fourth, having been engaged by the Duke of Athol to present a cast of Falcons to the king, that being the tenure by which the Dukes of Athol held the Isle of Man of the crown, viz. the presentation of a cast of Hawks at each coronation. There is an engraving of this picture also, but both are very scarce.

1819, and the grandfather was a celebrated Falconer. Peter Fleming, an ancestor, received a Hawk's Hood set with jewels from James IV. of Scotland, for beating the King's Falcon with his Tiercel. This interesting relic is carefully preserved in the family.

The Falconers employed by the Flemings have always been Scotchmen*.

Though Colonel Thornton's Falconers† were at first Dutch-

---

* Anderson was one of these Falconers; and being quite a character in the sporting world, and a very superior Falconer, a slight sketch of his life may be acceptable. He was born in the parish of Currie, on the estate of Mr. Scott of Mallaney, a few miles west of Edinburgh, about the year 1760. He commenced life by assisting his father, who was a tenant upon the Mallaney property, until he was twenty. He was then apprenticed to a currier in Edinburgh, and afterwards became his journeyman for some years. At length his love for the sports of the field, and particularly of Falconry (then common in Scotland), made him determine upon leaving his employer and becoming a Falconer. He was engaged by Mr. Fleming as Under Falconer, and soon afterwards succeeded John Hainshaw, who was the Head Falconer. He remained with Mr. Fleming until that gentleman's death, after which he appears to have retired to Ashfield, near Glasgow, where he died in 1833, at the advanced age of 84.

† Perhaps a short memoir of this celebrated sportsman may not be considered out of place here.

The country must have undergone a great change since Colonel Thornton lived at Thornville Royal, in Yorkshire, which he sold to Lord Stourton in 1805. Whilst residing there, the hawks were flown at Hack from the observatory in the park; and the present dairy, which is a tasteful building, was then the mews. The Colonel hawked over all the neighbouring moors, as Blubber House Moor, Grassington Moor, &c., and over the then open country about Kirk Deighton. At Beilby Grange (then called Wetherby Grange) there was a Heronry, and Clifford and Bramham Moor being then not enclosed, the Colonel flew at the Herons as they passed over these moors upon "the passage." Whilst the crops were standing, he used to sojourn to the Yorkshire Wolds, where he built a house near Boythorpe, which is twelve miles from Scarborough. He called this house "Falconer's Hall," and as the Wolds were then all in grass, he had nothing to interfere with his hawking. In 1808 he left Yorkshire for Spy Park in Wiltshire, which he took upon a lease.

There can be no doubt he left this open grass country about the time that the Yorkshire Wolds were broken up for corn-crops, which became so

men, he preferred the Scotch Falconers so much for the management of Eyesses, that he latterly always had a Scotchman for his head Falconer. Another instance of a Scotch Falconer we have in Thomas Kennedy of Mayboll in Ayrshire, who commenced the profession about 1761. He was long in the service of Lord O'Neil of Stanes Castle, County of Antrim *.

About the year 1812, Mr. Sinclair, of the Falls near Belfast, had a Scotch Falconer of the name of James Marshall (at that time about fifty years of age), who appears to have come from Lord Eglinton's service †. Lord Eglinton had many Falconers during his life, who were all Scotchmen, and wholly unconnected with the " Dutch school."

From the time of the civil wars we cannot trace Falconry satisfactorily in England; that is, we should fail if called upon to give a list of amateur Falconers from that time to about the close of the last century, from which period (the close of the eighteenth century) to the present day we could produce a very perfect list were it required. Notwithstanding this, there can be no doubt that this sport has always existed, of which we have sufficient evidence. For instance, the

---

valuable during the war. About 1814 he gave up keeping Hawks, and the year after he bought the Principality of Chambord and the Marquesite of Pont, and coming in to these titles, the Prince de Chambord spent the remainder of his life at his principality, enjoying the sports of wild-boar hunting, &c. to within a year or two of his death, which took place in his 75th year at Paris (where he often resided) in the spring of 1823, leaving a daughter, then six years old, to succeed him.

* Lord O'Neil was a famous Falconer. He used to take his Hawks from Ireland to Strathconnan, in Ross-shire, every year: as there were no houses then upon Scotch moors, he took a wooden one with him. Colonel Bonham, about 1840, took the same moors for hawking for some seasons. His Falconer was Francis M'Cullock.

† Campbell, the author of a work on Falconry, was an amateur Falconer, being a person of property, and not a professional one in the service of the Earl of Eglinton, as stated in Blaine's ' Encyclopedia of Rural Sports.'

Dukes of St. Albans have for ages been the hereditary Grand Falconers of England*.

There is no mention made in the Exchequer Records in Edinburgh of the Grand Falconers of Scotland; but the Under-Falconer's salary, &c. being often mentioned from an early period, we infer that the Head Falconer was but an honorary office. The last Under-Falconer was Mr. Marshall Gardener, who retired from his office in September 1840, since which time it has been in abeyance.

In the south-west of Scotland†, and probably also in Nor-folk (where the chalk formation‡ runs through the county), Falconry has remained stationary; in other localities it has ever been upon the ebb and flow. It is only some forty years since the introduction of a new system of agriculture into the county of Dorset, which has banished the Land-rails pre-viously abounding there, that taking these birds with Spar-row Hawks has been relinquished.

So completely has Falconry been given up upon the Con-tinent, that we know of but two instances for certain in which it is now practised. The first is that of the Loo Hawking

* We believe the Duke of St. Albans' Hawks have not been publicly exhibited since 1836, when they were frequently flown at Brighton.

† The Renfrewshire subscription Hawks were kept by Mr. Fleming of Baro-chan Tower, Renfrewshire, for many years, until his death in 1819. Amongst the many sportsmen who took a leading part in the Hawking-field along with Mr. Fleming, was Sir John Maxwell, Baronet, of Pollock, and the late Mr. Wal-lace of Kelly, formerly member for Greenock. In 1845, Sir John Maxwell en-gaged William Barr, Jun., then of Arrochar, as his private Falconer. Sir John dying two or three years after this, Barr commenced exhibiting his Hawks through England, which he continued to do for some seasons. He flew them at game when engaged by gentlemen, and on public occasions he flew them at pigeons upon race-grounds and other open places.

‡ It is always a good open Hawking country where the chalk approaches the surface, as well from the absence of timber and the weakness in the growth of the hedges, as also because much of it is still retained as permanent sheep walks, like the Berkshire and Wiltshire Downs, &c.

Club*, held annually at the Loo, in the neighbourhood of Arnheim, Apeldoorn†, Holland.

The second is that of a tribe of gipsies in Wallachia, near Bucharest, who, having to pay tribute to the Porte in the shape of many thousand quails, take them all by means of Sparrow Hawks. These Hawks are caught in nets while migrating, and after being trained are used in the capture of the required number of quails, after which they are restored to liberty.

We suspect that in some parts of Russia this sport is still pursued, as we have been informed by Colonel Wilson Patten, M.P. for North Lancashire, that in the year 1825 he met with Hawking in that country. Colonel Wilson Patten witnessed Hawking as one of the amusements at the coronation of the late Emperor. He also met with it while on a visit to Prince Sapieha, and as his account of the sport is interesting we are glad to insert it. There is seldom any possibility of approaching partridges with a gun, upon the open country, which so frequently extends for miles in Russia, and therefore the sportsmen adopt the following expedient.

Horsemen, accompanied by Hawks on the wing, and bearing poles, at the top of which are fixed small round platforms, where the Hawks have been taught to look for their food, ride over the ground considerably in advance of the shooting party; from time to time they fix these poles in the earth and allow the Hawks to light upon them, which they readily do in the absence of all trees, and upon the approach of the shooters they proceed forwards as before. The game being terrified at

---

* This club, consisting of fifty members, and under the patronage of the King of Holland, with His Royal Highness Prince Alexander of Holland at its head, was established in the year 1838. It has many English members. Those who took great interest in getting it up were the Duke of Leeds, the late Honourable Charles Wortley, and Mr. Newcome. Adrian Mollen is the Head Falconer.

† About the year 1840, Prince Trautmansdorf kept Passage Hawks for some two or three seasons near Vienna, where he had good Rook and Heron Hawking.

the sight of the Hawks, lie beautifully to the dogs of the advancing sportsmen. The same gentleman also mentioned that when the Falcons happen to be lost near a forest, they are brought up by the sound of a large bell, to which they have been accustomed at feeding-time. A similar mode of making grouse lie to the gun, when very wild, is sometimes practised in this country—a kite made to resemble a Hawk being used in the place of the living bird; it is a practice however which scarcely comes within the bounds of legitimate sport.

Hawking is the national sport of Syria, Persia, and many parts of India, as the valley of the Indus*, &c. From skins which have reached this country from China and Japan, evidently those of trained birds, it is certain that Falconry is practised also there. Travellers likewise speak of having met with it amongst the Moors in Africa. In the New World it is quite unknown.

The decline of a sport once so generally practised in this country may be attributed to several causes; the principal one having no doubt in the first instance arisen from the more frequent use of gunpowder: this, and the enclosing of waste lands, gave the first blow to the art. A great reaction with regard to the Hawks themselves followed, and in place of the strict protection they used to enjoy came a most violent persecution. Discarded as allies in the field, they were and are only looked upon as enemies; and the same noble bird, which in former days would have rested on a monarch's wrist, is now handed over to the tender mercies of a menial as *vermin*. The custom of collecting together within narrow bounds large quantities of game, artificially reared, and semi-domesticated, has tended greatly of late years to destroy the taste for *real* sport amongst the upper orders, and at the same time to crowd the gaols from the lower ranks of

* See Lieut. Burton on Hawking in the Valley of the Indus. Van Voorst, Paternoster Row.

society. No pursuit deserves the title of sport, which taxes nothing beyond the organ of destruction in those who follow it. The Battue system, in which hundreds of pheasants reared almost by the hand of the keeper, and scores of hares enclosed within nets, are driven into the very faces of *sportsmen* posted in advantageous situations, and slaughtered by wholesale with the smallest possible expenditure of trouble to the slayers, may be styled in newspaper paragraphs " glorious day's sport *," but has certainly nothing in common with that description of sport which brings into play the qualities of energy, perseverance, endurance of fatigue, great self-command, and calmness of nerve in times of difficulty, and which has given to the national character its title to respect, in the sportsman by flood and field at home, and the warrior abroad. One part of this system of game-preserving consists in the destruction of every bird or beast supposed capable of claiming its share in the spoil, whether or not nature has provided it with the requisite powers or even inclination. As might be imagined, this mode of arriving at the desired end generally defeats itself, and the extirpation of one supposed hostile species only makes way for some other still more destructive agent; as for instance, in localities where everything in the shape of weasel, stoat, or foumart, has disappeared, immense numbers of rats, equally destructive to game, and far more generally injurious, have sprung up, and from their amazing fertility defy the skill of man to hunt them down. An excess of birds and beasts of prey, generally called in gamekeeper's language " *vermin*," no one would advocate; there is, however, no doubt that such may be killed off far too closely; it is a dangerous thing to break the admirable balance of nature, and were the habits of the greater number

---

* Somewhat equivalent to this, is the wholesale slaughter of sea fowl which annually takes place at Flamborough Head and other breeding places, where the birds are mercilessly shot in hundreds and their bodies left floating upon the waves.

of our larger Hawks better known, it would be found that instead of being injurious to the preservation of game, exactly the opposite is the case. Though gamekeepers are in general a prejudiced race, and probably draw their conclusions as to the usual prey of the Hawks they meet with, from seeing them in the act of discussing the remains of one of their own victims, it is but fair to remark, that we know more than one of their number, who, being observing and intelligent men, rejoice in a visit from the Peregrine to their moors during the time that the grouse are laying; being aware that the Falcon's principal object of pursuit at that season is the Royston and carrion crow, and other egg-stealers which then infest the ground. On some of the Highland moors the alpine hares have become so numerous, in consequence of the destruction of their chief enemy the Golden Eagle*, as to prove a perfect nuisance both to the farmer and also to the sportsman, whose dogs are continually pointing them.

In addition to this mistaken persecution, all our large and rare birds are disappearing from a more legitimate cause, viz. the increase of a taste for objects of natural history, and more particularly for collecting eggs. Every village has now its bird-stuffer, whose trade is supplied by the gun of every idle fellow in the country. Unfortunately also writers on zoology as well as botany have been in the habit of publishing the exact localities of rare specimens, which has led to the entire extermination of the objects of their regard by professional collectors, who scruple not to carry off everything that will sell, provided they are the gainers for the time.

* Falconers have discovered that there are three obstacles which make it perfectly useless to attempt to train the Golden Eagle. These are, its powers of fasting, and when it is sufficiently hungry to fly, its inability to turn quickly, owing to the shape of its wings; and lastly, its sulky disposition should it miss its quarry. Eagles catch by "grabbing" or "clutching" with their feet, so that probably in their wild state they sweep down from the clouds during windy weather (wind being a great assistance to them) and pick off their victims from the ground.

We cannot dismiss this subject without expressing a hope that the good taste of some noblemen and gentlemen, who, observing the motto "live and let live," preserve the eyries of the Golden Eagle and Peregrine on their properties (and do not perceive one head of game less in consequence), may be more generally imitated; this alone can prevent such noble birds from shortly becoming extinct.

It is to employers we must look for rectifying the prevailing system of destruction, it being needless to expect that servants, without directions from their masters, will desist from a practice in which they have been brought up, and taught to consider the principal part of their duty, and in many instances are paid expressly for its performance; and which, even if not on their master's account, they carry on for their own benefit, it being a common practice for country bird-stuffers to contract to take everything in the shape of hawk, owl, jay, kingfisher, woodpecker, &c., with which the neighbouring gamekeepers can supply them. Sorry as we should be to see the legitimate taste for natural history decline, it must more or less disappear with the objects of its pursuit; for in nature, unlike the world of commerce, demand and supply do not keep pace; the former, instead of creating, destroys the latter; and without the protecting aid of those who alone can adequately afford it, all that is most interesting to the zoologist in this country will soon vanish.

The following excellent remarks regarding the qualifications necessary in a Falconer we have met with somewhere, and cannot do wrong in giving them :—

"A Falconer will frequently have to follow his Hawks on horseback, as well as upon foot, and should consequently be a good horseman. He should possess strength, health, and courage, or, in other words, he should be 'a sinewy son of nature,' to enable him to bear the fatigues of running, leaping, ascending hills, dashing through rivers and fields flooded by winter's rain, of pressing through thickets, and of surmounting the many other difficulties that may present themselves. Agility is also requisite, that he may be able to attend his Hawks in their flights, and serve them with game whilst they are making their aërial circlings above his head, in keen expectation of it. As they will often outfly his utmost speed, his voice should be full, clear, and loud, in order to bring them back to the scene of action. They demand great regularity in their feeding and exercise, and that he may be seldom tempted to neglect it, he must be temperate in his living and methodical in all things, ever remembering this excellent motto, ' Order is gain : have a place for everything, and keep all in its place.' His love for the sport should be most intense, to animate him to undergo, undaunted, the numberless inconveniences of attendance, weather, and toil, wherewith it is generally accompanied. His main pleasure should be, to be always with his Hawks—training them to obedience, correcting their faults, and consulting their health and beauty. To do these things effectually, he must understand their different tempers and constitutions, and should possess much patience and mildness in the application of this knowledge. Hawks, under the management of a man thus qualified, will be always in good order for flying, exhibit the greatest boldness and address in coursing their prey, give the highest pleasure to the beholders of their various evolutions, and do just honour to the skill and attention of their keeper."

" Decision, strength, agility, keenness and diligence, which are indispensably necessary to the menial Falconer, ought also to be found in the master whom he serves. They enable him to bear his part in the sport with becoming manliness, to derive from it all the amusement it can give, and to overawe his servant into the honest and regular discharge of his duty."

THE COUNTRY REQUISITE FOR THE SPORT.

Almost all field-sports require a peculiar style of country. For Falconry, one suitable to it is absolutely necessary. Nothing, not even the importunities of friends, should tempt a Falconer to fly his Hawk in a bad situation; for without a chance of sport, he will either lose his bird entirely, or at least spend an anxious day in searching for her. A district fitted for this amusement * cannot be too open or flat; for as the powerful flight of the Falcon gives her the advantage over her prey, she must have scope for the exercise of that power. In their wild state these noble birds are only met with in the most open countries, and it is as impossible for them to kill in an enclosed country, as it is for a greyhound to course in a wood. For Heron and Rook Hawking, which embrace the higher branches of the art, an actual plain, particularly if *in grass*, is desirable. Upon grass, rooks may generally be found; the ground is the very best to ride over, and there is the additional advantage of being able to carry on the sport at all seasons, which, on account of the standing crops, cannot be done elsewhere. When Hawking is pursued in a cultivated country, the fields ought to be very large, with either the weak ill-grown fences found upon a bad soil (particularly

---

* Whenever Hawking is commenced in a country where it is a new sport, it should be previously made as public as possible, otherwise persons who are ignorant of it might shoot the Hawks. There are many ways of making the thing known. This may be done by an advertisement in the newspapers, by a public day's Hawking, and by putting out notices in public places on public occasions, &c. The Notice may be drawn up to this effect :—

NOTICE.

The Public are respectfully requested by

———————— of ————

not to shoot or injure his TRAINED HAWKS

which are flown in this neighbourhood.

N.B. A Trained Hawk may be known by having bells and straps to its legs.

over the chalk-formation where it approaches the surface), or with the low, neatly trimmed hedges which the improved method of modern agriculture has introduced, being opposed as it is to all hedge-row timber, wide fences, and small enclosures. The best grass districts are to be met with about East Ilsley in Berkshire, Amesbury, Warminster, and Lavington near Devizes, all in Wiltshire*, and the Curragh of Kildare near Newbridge in Ireland. There must be a good Hawking country upon Dartmoor in Devonshire, also about Portsmouth, Southampton, Winchester, and Bagshot Heath. About Hitchin in Hertfordshire the ground is sufficiently open, near which is yet to be seen the ditch where Henry VIII. nearly lost his life, by the breaking of his hawking pole. The neighbourhood of Peterborough in Northamptonshire is a fine suitable district, as likewise the country about Feltwell, Hockwold, and Didlington in Norfolk, about Newmarket in Cambridgeshire, Sleaford in Lincolnshire, and about Rainford near Wigan in Lancashire, &c. The Yorkshire Wolds are now generally strongly fenced and intersected with larch plantations; this has spoilt the country for Hawking; in some few places, however, the ground still remains open. There is an excellent country for this sport almost all along the east coast of Scotland, as far as to Inverness; as also on the south-west in Renfrew, Ayr, Wigtonshire, &c. There are other immense tracts of moorland highly fitted for grouse hawking in particular, such as the neighbourhood of Strathconnan in Ross-shire, where Lord O'Neill, and after his day Colonel Bonham, kept their Hawks during the autumn months †. In like manner Colonel Thornton had his birds for one season at Raits upon the Spey in Inverness-shire ‡.

---

* These are the South Downs; the cultivated country adjoining these downs also affords excellent Hawking ground after the harvest.

† See Mr. Knox's excellent little work entitled 'Game Birds and Wild Fowl, their Friends and their Foes,' p. 161.

‡ Colonel Thornton's 'Northern Tour.'

In Ireland, at Castle Martin, halfway between Kildare and Monastereven, there is a Heronry, and a marsh on which Herons have been taken by Mr. O'Keefe. Between Sugarloaf Hill and Roundwood, County of Wicklow, there is also a marsh called Caleny, upon which herons, grouse, rooks, and plovers have been taken by the same gentleman, who speaks highly of the woodcock hawking on the Wicklow mountains early in the season; he also names a bog and moor near Banagher in King's County, for heron hawking, and good partridge hawking near the Black Bull, at Rathreagan, County of Meath.

THE EXPENSE OF A HAWKING ESTABLISH-MENT.

Though Hawking may be enjoyed in a quiet way at a very trifling expense, where only a cast or a cast and a half of Hawks are kept, a regular Hawking establishment would incur a considerable expenditure. For this purpose, about eight Hawks would be necessary, as also a Falconer and his assistant, with one or two good horses and three or four dogs; so that, calculating the wages of the Falconer and his assistant, and the keep of the horses, dogs, and hawks *, we may put it down at not less than £200 a-year.

---

* When a Hawk is moulting and is not kept upon what it kills in the field, as rooks, &c., it will require about a third of a pound of fresh beef daily, and occasionally in the place of beef it is necessary to give it warm food, as a live pigeon twice a week.

CHAPTER I.

THE EYESS OR NESTLING PEREGRINE—TAKING FROM THE NEST, REARING, AND FLYING AT HACK.

THE Peregrine, together with one or two very closely allied species, has at all times, and in every country where the art of Falconry is practised, been most highly valued for its docility, swiftness, courage, and hardiness of constitution; it is found more widely distributed than perhaps any other bird; specimens from North America, China, Australia, as well as Africa, are not distinguishable from those found in our own country, and have in all probability no specific difference. These islands appear to be a favourite resort of this noble bird, as, when allowed to remain in peace, almost every precipitous headland, as well as inaccessible inland crag, is the abode of a pair during the spring and summer months. The constant persecution to which it is so generally exposed, has unfortunately of late years rendered barren many a crag which formerly year after year produced a favourite eyrie. Were the habits of this bird better known, this persecution (from which, if only for the sake of "*auld lang syne*," it might have been exempted) would probably be changed again into protection. On the sea-coast its prey consists almost entirely of water-birds, or the wild rock pigeons, which likewise select similar situations as itself for breeding in; while, inland, the benefit it does to the game-preserver, in clearing those moors over which its range extends, of carrion and Royston crows, magpies, and other egg- and chicken-hunting marauders, far more than compensates him for the few head of game it may in the course of the year appropriate. This species of Hawk strikes its prey always on the wing, and as all Falconers know the difficulty of making grouse and other game rise, even with the assistance of dogs, while their enemy is in sight, it can only be occasionally, and then, often, when the birds are either wounded or sickly, that the wild Falcon* gets a chance of making its stroke: this is not the case with its usual objects of attack, such as gulls, plovers, rooks, wild pigeons, &c., which attempt to escape their foe by strength of wing. One or both of the parent birds may be seen during the time that the young require their care, in constant activity, screaming, circling, and dashing from a height in pursuit of the weaker, or repelling with the greatest boldness the approach of more powerful intruders on their domain. Only one eyrie will be found within a certain district, the most powerful birds suffering no rival to share in their hunting grounds. The time for taking the young birds from the nest differs according to locality and season; we have known an eyrie, from which the young birds flew on the 26th of May, whereas they are frequently not ready until the 10th to the 20th of June. The longer the young remain with the parent birds the better, and in no case should they be taken until the white down with which they are at first covered has in a great measure been re-placed by feathers, those of the tail being not less than 3 inches in length; for, if taken at an earlier age, they are almost certain to fall victims to the "cramp," either within a day or two after leaving the nest, or at some period before they are fully fledged. We have, however, known a young bird even make an attempt to fly before the fatal paroxysm seized it. In all cases where this disease attacks the young Hawk, (and it can immediately be known by the peculiar scream of agony with which the convulsion is accompanied,) the most merciful

---

* The Peregrine Falcon is provincially known by several names, as the "Hunting Hawk." In Ireland and in North America it is called the Duck Hawk; and on the south coast of England, about the Isle of Wight, it is known as the *Broad Arrow*, from its assuming that form in its perpendicular stoop.

plan is to destroy the sufferer at once : the powerful contraction of the muscles affected always either bends or breaks the then soft bones to which they are attached; and even should the bird survive, it becomes perfectly useless, as the wing-bones are the parts first affected in the young Peregrine; in most cases it dies after some days' torture, when the bones of both wings and legs will be found to be broken in several places. By watching the eyrie with the aid of a glass, it is easily ascertained when the young Hawks are fit to be taken.

In many localities where the nest is on the sea-coast, there are persons in the neighbourhood accustomed to descend the cliffs in search of sea-birds and their eggs; these are the best parties to employ for taking the young Hawks, as, to those unaccustomed to the sort of thing, there is great risk in making the attempt. Where, however, such cragsmen cannot be met with, every precaution should be taken to avoid an accident. A light man or boy of good nerve should be chosen for going over the cliff. Having sufficient force, and an excellent new rope (not too thick), which has previously been stretched, and had the turns taken out of it, make what is called a *" bowline knot on a bight "* (Pl. XXIV. fig. 2), which forms a double loop, and also a smaller one at the knot, which secures the person round the waist, leaving the arms at liberty; by sitting either on the double loop at the bottom, or by thrusting each leg through one of these loops (the smaller loop at the knot having been first passed over the shoulders, securing the waist), all danger of the party slipping from the rope would be avoided;—a second rope had better be attached in the same manner for greater safety. The principal danger arises from the falling of loose stones detached by the rope; these the pendent party ought as much as possible to remove before passing them; he should also wear a padded cap, or some similar protection for the head. He must take with him a covered basket, having straw at the bottom, and attached by a small line to the man who

manages the ropes at the top of the rock; in this basket the
young Hawks are raised, as soon as secured. The line may
also be used as a signal by the man below, should he wish to
call the attention of his friends above. All being ready, two
or more strong men are to hold the ropes, while another on
the edge of the precipice guides them, giving directions as to
lowering or raising the man below: as soon as the nest is
reached (the exact situation of which should be previously
well ascertained), the young Hawks* are to be placed as
gently as possible in the basket, great care being taken not
to injure them in their then tender state, raised to the top,
and fed as soon as everything is safe. Many Falconers make
arrangements to have the young Hawks sent to them, often
from a considerable distance; when this is the case, it is of
the utmost importance that the birds should be so fed and
packed as to reach their future owner in good order, as much
of their usefulness for the first year depends upon the treatment they receive at the hands of those who take charge of
them from the nest:—in all cases we should say, handle them
as little as possible, place them where they cannot injure
themselves, on short straw or clean stable litter, being careful
to keep their bedding in a clean state, and feed them *three*
times a day on fresh raw beef, free from fat and skin, or with
fresh-killed rabbits, pigeons, rooks, or other birds, giving
them on each occasion as much as they will eat, the food
being cut into small pieces. For travelling, line the sides of
a hamper with matting to protect the young feathers, and be
careful to feed the birds immediately before starting. They
should travel if possible at night, and always by the quickest

---

* We have known young Hawks successfully taken from the nest when in an
awkward situation by means of a fishing-rod, with a noose of horsehair at the
end of it. Upon the birds feeling this, they immediately seize the end of the rod
with their feet, and are thus safely raised. When there is danger of their flying
off, from their being too far advanced, a landing net is of great use to put over
them as they sit in the nest.

mode of conveyance, as a few hours' delay, and consequent starvation, will produce a permanent injury.

Young Hawks may be reared in different ways; Sir John Sebright recommends that they should be placed upon clean straw in a large hamper, firmly fixed about breast high against a tree, in a retired situation; by means of two strings the lid of the hamper may be so supported from each side as to form a sort of platform for the young birds to come out upon when they are fed; they should be sheltered from the rain by means of a piece of oil-cloth; the sides of the hamper protect the birds from the wind, and they may be placed so as to receive the sun. Some Falconers prefer keeping them upon straw, on the ground, within a large barn or other building, the door being left open during the day to allow the young Hawks to come out and look about them. They soon learn to distinguish the voice and whistle of the Falconer, and only require regular feeding at fixed hours, which should be at first three times a day; after they can fly, and as long as they are kept at hack, twice a day, morning and evening; whatever food they leave being entirely removed.

Sir John Sebright explains so well a disease to which young Hawks at this time are liable, that we shall give it in his own words :—

"There is frequently to be observed in the plumage of birds of prey a defect, which goes by the name of *hunger traces*, owing to want of food at some period during the growth of the feathers *. Though the full-grown Falcon, when in health, may bear without injury the long fasts incident to birds of prey, the young Eyess suffers, like the young of all other animals, from deficiency of nourishment; and the consequence is principally discernible in the feathers. This defect, when strongly marked, may be seen in some degree on every feather of the body, but it is especially observable on the expanded wing or tail, in a line crossing all the

---

* Ill-fed sheep have a similar disease in their wool.

feathers. On the shaft of each feather the mark may not only be seen, but felt, as a ridge slightly projecting. It may also be seen as a line of imperfection across the web of every feather, neatly marked as if a razor had been lightly passed across the wing. The injury from this cause is sometimes such as to occasion the feathers to break off at the hunger-trace; and it is not improbable that the razor-mark seen on the web is in fact owing to the breaking off of all the fine fibres of the web in the line of the trace."

To avoid this defect in the plumage, it is only necessary to take care that the young Hawks are regularly and plentifully fed; they should have at each meal as much as they can be induced to take, and the younger they are, the more easy of digestion should their food be. When fully grown and in constant exercise, nothing agrees with them better than fresh, but lean, raw beef, together with a few mouthfuls daily of feathers or fur to produce "castings;" at an earlier age, however, they seem to require a lighter diet; and the flesh of fresh-killed birds or rabbits at every other meal is preferable to beef alone. Sir John Sebright recommends that raw eggs should be mixed with their food two or three times a week, as a means of making the feathers broad and strong. They should be fed as much as possible from the hand of the Falconer, the food being given to them in small pieces; great care being at the same time taken to prevent them acquiring the habit of flying away with portions of the food, which is called "*carrying*;" this being a fault to which all Hawks are inclined, and which when once acquired it is very difficult to correct. As soon as they can fly well, they may be fed occasionally upon the lure, pieces of meat being fastened thereon for the purpose, the Falconer at the same time giving them a few morsels from his hand, and accustoming them to his voice and whistle.

The best situations for flying Hawks at hack are from old buildings near rocks and cliffs conspicuously placed in an open country, where there are but few inhabitants; as, however, there is always danger of the birds being destroyed either wilfully or through ignorance, especially when they extend their flights to a considerable distance, public notices, as recommended at p. 16 of Introduction, had better be put up, requesting all those who meet with them to avoid doing them any injury; and generally speaking this precaution, with the addition of a bell upon each bird, will ensure their safety.

As it is very desirable to keep the young Hawks for some weeks in this state of liberty, as soon as they are strong on the wing, large bells, or leaden weights, covered with soft wash-leather, should be fastened to their legs, to prevent their preying for themselves; otherwise it will be necessary to take them up, as soon as their absence from the accustomed feeding-place for a day or two shows that they have learnt to help themselves. This is easily accomplished by means of a small bow net (*vide* Plate XXIV. fig. 3) baited with a piece of meat, or even by a noose of soft cord placed round the food fastened to the ground, and which is drawn over the legs of the Hawk whilst it is feeding.

Should nestlings be too far advanced before they reach the Falconer to be trusted at once at hack, they had better be provided with jesses, swivel and leash, and placed on the block, until they have become tolerably tame, and acquainted with their feeder; after this they may be weighted, as before mentioned, and turned out. In this way also even old Hawks * may be kept at hack; when this is done, they should be fed in the morning before they are turned loose.

* Old Hawks acquire a wonderful knowledge of locality, as well as instinctive regard for the place where they are kept; so much so, that if their home is conspicuously situated in an open country, they will return to it after having been lost for a time in the neighbourhood. We could mention several curious facts of this kind, but perhaps one will suffice. This remarkable instance occurred in the case of an old Falcon belonging to Colonel Bonham. The bird broke loose in the north of Ireland during last spring, and returned home after an absence of a month.

Some Falconers take up their young Hawks as soon as they are strong upon the wing, and after having tamed, trained, and entered them at some quarry, turn them out at hack again. Others feed them off the lure, and taking them in at night, place them in a dark room. Under these systems the birds may be kept a long time at liberty.

Before trusting old Hawks to fly at hack with the young ones, it is necessary to know their tempers, some birds being so hot-tempered as to be continually " crabbing," whilst others will even kill their weaker companions. Smaller species, such as Merlins, are never safe where Peregrines are at large; care must also be taken, when the Hawks are confined to their blocks, that they do not reach each other. This system of flying young Hawks at hack * is indispensable in the case of all the Falcons, as it not only gives them power of wing, without which they are valueless, but also teaches them to return to the place from whence they are started, after an unsuccessful flight. With the short-winged Hawks, however, it is not necessary, as their flights are only for a short distance, and they are seldom out of sight of the Falconer.

If there should not be a stream near at hand wherein the " hack Hawks " can bathe, a bath must be sunk in the ground for their use, and regularly filled.

Falconers differ in opinion respecting the mode of forming a Mews †. Some like it to consist of a long, low building, enclosed at the sides, having one or two doors, and

* We believe that hawks are not flown at hack in the East, certainly not in Syria : the native Falconers admit the advantages to be derived from the system, but say that it cannot be done there, as the hawks would certainly be stolen.

† The Mews at Charing Cross was established in 1377 by Richard II., and continued to be used as such until the year 1537, when in the 27th of Henry VIII.'s reign it was converted into the king's stables. All stables in London are now called Mews, which is evidently a corruption of the places used for keeping and moulting Hawks in, Mews being derived from *muto*, to change.—Blain's Encyclopædia of Rural Sports.

a window with a shutter, so that the whole may be made dark at any time. In this building the Hawks' blocks are placed upon a bed of sand 6 inches deep, which both absorbs the mutes, and at the same time prevents the feathers of the Hawks which bate from being broken. Straw is also used sometimes instead of sand for the same purpose; both require to be kept clean. Other Falconers prefer keeping their Hawks as much as possible in their natural state, and place them upon grass in a sheltered situation, with the addition, however, of a shed, open on all sides, to protect them in some measure during very bad weather, or when it is an object to keep their feathers dry.

Others keep their birds exposed day and night at all seasons; as, however, Hawks in their wild state would certainly select sheltered situations during stormy weather, it must be in accordance with nature, as well as humanity, to provide them, while in captivity, with a similar indulgence. During severe weather Hawks require an extra allowance of food; if this is not attended to, they will rapidly lose flesh and become diseased; while in high condition, however, they can endure without injury a great degree of cold, and will bathe as usual with the thermometer below the freezing-point. Everything about the mews should be kept perfectly clean. The birds soon learn to know the voice and even the step * of the Falconer; some, however, will remain shy and suspicious should he but change his dress; it is an advantage therefore to keep as much as possible to one costume.

In colour the young Peregrine differs considerably from the adult bird. During the first year the plumage is brown, the feathers of the back and wings being edged with a lighter tint; the breast and thighs are more or less rufous, with dark brown longitudinal streaks. Whilst in the nest, and for some little time after leaving it, the young birds have a bluish

* A kite kept for some years by one of the authors, always recognized the approach of its master by a peculiar low cry before seeing him.

slate-coloured bloom over the darker parts of the body, which gives them some resemblance in colour to their parents; as soon however as they begin to bathe, this bloom disappears, and they become quite brown. Like all other birds, they differ much in intensity of colour, being found both of light and dark varieties, with the intermediate shades. The colour of the cere and eyelids is at first blue, which generally changes by degrees to a yellow tint *, and by the end of the first year becomes bright yellow, provided the bird be in health; the tarsi and feet from the first are light yellow, acquiring depth of colour by age. After the first moult the brown plumage is replaced by one of a blue slate-colour, approaching to black on the head, wings and tail, whilst the longitudinal streaks on the breast and thighs give place to transverse bars.

The Falcons, or Long-winged Hawks, are distinguished from the true or Short-winged Hawks by three never-failing characteristics: viz. by the tooth on the upper mandible (this in some of the foreign species is doubled), by the second feather of the wing being either the longest or equal in length to the third, and by the nature of the stoop made in pursuit of their prey.

* We knew an instance of it changing to yellow in one night.

CHAPTER II.

MODE OF TRAINING THE EYESS PEREGRINE, WITH THE IMPLEMENTS, ETC. USED.

In the former chapter we left the young Falcon just taken up from hack, and ready to commence the system of training necessary to prepare it for the field. Provided care has been taken during the time the bird was at liberty to accustom it to the call of the Falconer to feed from his hand, and also to understand the lure, very little will remain to be done, beyond getting it to sit quietly on the fist, and also to bear the hood without resistance; this may be accomplished in the course of a few days, and within a week it ought to be again exercising its powers of flight; as, however, so much depends upon the disposition of each bird and the skill of the trainer, we should always recommend young Falconers to avoid anything like hurrying on the education of their Hawks (this is particularly necessary in the case of adult wild-caught birds), as much labour and time are often lost by so doing. Carrying the young Hawk as much as possible on the fist, and accustoming it to the presence of strangers, as also horses, dogs, &c., is the most efficacious mode of rendering it quickly docile and fearless: called in technical language, "manning" it. It is astonishing in how short a space of time these birds cease to pay the least attention to sights or sounds, of whatever description they may be; we have even witnessed one disregard the rush of a railway train passing within a few feet; and on occasions when the sport has been publicly exhibited during the last three or four years, the birds (principally young ones) employed for the purpose appeared not to notice the presence of many hundred noisy spectators.

Before, however, describing further the system of training usually practised, we will endeavour to explain the various articles employed in the process.

The *Jesses* consist of narrow strips of some very tough leather fastened on to the Hawk's legs, by which it is held; these are generally put on before the bird is allowed to fly at *hack*. The best leather for the purpose is the white leather used by saddlers; it is made from horse-hide, tanned in alum and salt, and when well greased is remarkably tough and durable, and as it can be procured of any thickness, may be used for the different species of Hawk. Dog-skin regularly tanned is also sometimes made use of, as well as a strong calf-leather called by shoemakers "kip." In every case great care is necessary in selecting for the purpose thoroughly sound leather, as a valuable bird may be easily lost by neglect in this particular. For the mode of fastening the jesses on to the bird's legs, *vide* Plate XXII. fig. 9

Formerly small flat silver or brass rings, called varvels, were attached to the loose end of the jesses, on which was engraved the owner's name and address. The use of these is at the present day in a great measure discontinued, as they both add to the weight the bird has to carry, and also to the chance of the jesses becoming entangled in trees*; the owner's name can be as easily engraved on the bell.

When the Hawk is fastened to its block, a swivel made of iron or brass is put on the jesses by means of the slit in the ends (*vide* Plate XXII. fig. 10). Both jesses being fastened to one loop of the swivel, through the other loop, the leash made of strong white or "kip" leather, with a button at its thickest end, is passed, and fastened to an iron pin in the ground close to the block, by what is called the Falconer's knot (*vide* Plate XXIII. fig. 5). Sometimes the leash is attached to a staple in the block itself, instead of to a pin;

---

* One of the authors had a fine Falcon very much injured by an accident of this sort.

the latter however is the preferable mode, provided the pin is very firm in the ground. The leash should be about two feet in length; the button is formed by folding the broad end of the leather, punching a hole through the folds, and then drawing the smaller end and the whole remaining length of the leash through. When the Hawk is flown, the swivel* and leash are taken off, the jesses and bell † always remaining on the bird. Bells are of the greatest use in finding a Hawk that has killed its game, at some distance from the Falconer, particularly where the ground is rough, as amongst brackens, turnips, &c.; also for discovering the haunts of a strayed Hawk; and, when good, they can be heard at a considerable distance, particularly at night. Bells ‡ should be made as light as possible, and should be cast in one piece, as being then less liable to break than when two semispheres are soldered together. They are sometimes made of silver, or of German silver. Those of brass §, however, give the clearest sound. Falconers generally fasten the bell to the leg, or legs of their Hawks, above the jesses, by narrow strips of leather called *bewits* (*vide* Plate XXII. figs. 6 & 9). Some, however, prefer the Chinese mode of fixing it to the two middle feathers of the tail. This is best done by having the bell made with a long shank, the slit of which should project away from the body of the bell, instead of in the usual mode; through this slit a piece of whalebone, stiff leather, or gutta-percha, is passed (*vide* Plate XXII. figs. 7 & 8), by means of which the

* The best swivels we have seen were made by Westley Richard's agent, Mr. Bishop, 170 New Broad Street, London.

† Bells may be procured of Messrs. R. & E. Repp, 40, 41, 42 Chandos Street, Covent Garden, London.

‡ In olden times the best Hawk bells were made on the Continent, being imported into this country from Germany. In the 'Booke of St. Albans' we are told that the Milan Hawk bells were so made, that one bell was a semitone higher than the other.

§ A bell of rough manufacture, but of excellent tone, we met with lately upon the tail of a trained Peregrine (in the skin) from China.

bell is attached to the shafts of the feathers ; a hole sufficiently large to receive each shaft having been punched in the leather on each side of the shank, and tied firmly together when on by means of a wax-end.   Bells when fixed in this manner are from their position less liable to injury, and at the same time leave the leg and foot of the bird more free for its powerful blows: in the case of the Goshawk and Sparrow Hawk it is by far the best mode of applying them, as these birds are very apt to crouch and not stir their legs when upon their prey, although their long tails are in constant motion.   With the Peregrine this is not so much the case, as Falcons are continually scratching off the feathers of their quarry from their beak and eyes whilst eating, and, in so doing, ring the bell on the leg loudly.

The bell can be fastened on to the Hawk's leg whilst on the fist, hooded.   When, however, it is to be put on to the tail, the bird must be held by assistants during the operation; one should hold it firmly with its breast on a soft pillow, whilst a second secures its legs.   The thumbs of the first assistant ought to rest in the channel of the bird's back, and with his fingers prevent the wings from moving.   The mode of putting all these things on to the bird will be seen by reference to the Illustrations.

The blocks and stands upon which Hawks usually rest are made in different ways : that in most general use is formed of some hard wood in the shape of an inverted flower-pot (see Plate II.); for a Peregrine this block should be about a foot in height, six inches in diameter at the top, and nine at the base, to prevent its being overturned.   An iron spike* may be driven into the centre of the bottom of the block, which, running into the ground, keeps it firm.   For facility in moving, a ring may be counter-sunk into the top of the block. If a hole is bored quite through the wood of the block,

* These spikes may be made to screw on and off, and are then more convenient for travelling.

it will be less liable to split. When travelling, large round stones or flower-pots make very good blocks, the Hawks being tied to iron pins with eyes to them, which pins are driven into the ground near the pots.

The blocks that are placed under cover should be padded on the top, to prevent the Hawks' feet from becoming swollen, a disease they are very apt to acquire if kept at all times on a hard surface.

The block for Merlins should be made somewhat in the shape of a wine-glass, about 9 inches in height and 4 inches in diameter at the top, tapering off to an iron spike at the bottom, by which it is fixed in the ground, and on which it should be made to revolve. The leash is fastened to a staple about half-way down the block. This form of block is necessary with these little birds, in order to keep their plumage free from the mutes which they are liable to drop upon one of the usual shape. Some Falconers, however, prefer keeping their Merlins upon the perch or screen (*vide* Plate VII.), which is used also for Goshawks and Sparrow Hawks, and occasionally for Passage Hawks*. To this perch they are fastened by means of a very short leash, or by passing the button through a slit in the leash, and then bringing the latter round the perch where it is tied; the swivel rests upon the top of the perch, the Hawks having merely the length of their jesses, so that in bating off they cannot possibly touch the ground with the points of their wings, and also can the more easily regain their position. In order to assist the birds in doing this, canvas is nailed, so as to hang below the perch, and is drawn tight by being fastened also to the bottom of the stand or floor. It must be observed, however, that the perch should never be used for Eyess Peregrines, as it has been found that they are less active than Passage Hawks, and

---

* Merlins which are very quiet may be kept on the perch with safety even out of doors. Other hawks are liable to bate off, and get hung, except when hooded, or in a darkened room.

consequently that they are apt to hang themselves, that is, bate off, and not regain their position, in which case they soon die.

The Assyrian Hawk-stand (*vide* Plate XXI.) (for the introduction of which we are indebted to Mr. Barker) is well adapted to the Goshawk and Sparrow Hawk. For the former of these birds it should be made strong and heavy, about 18 inches square; two of the opposite sides of solid wood should be 3 inches in thickness and 11 inches deep; each of the remaining sides is formed of two round bars 2 inches in diameter, the lower one about $3\frac{1}{2}$ inches from the bottom, and the upper, upon which the bird perches, 4 inches above the other. Upon each of these bars are rings, to any of which the Hawk may be fastened. For a Sparrow Hawk the stand should be 14 inches square and 8 inches deep, with the bars 3 inches apart. In order to prevent the leash from getting under the stand, or the Hawk from moving it, it is better to sink it a little into the ground.

The most simple mode, however, of securing these short-winged Hawks is upon the bow perch (*vide* Plate XX.). This perch is made from a piece of ash, bent in hot water, and kept in its position by means of a strong wire, a ring of somewhat larger diameter than the bow having been previously put on: the ends of the wood should be shod with iron spikes for fixing it into the ground. For a Goshawk a bow about 3 inches in diameter will be sufficient; half that size for a Sparrow Hawk.

All the blocks and perches that are exposed to the weather should be well painted.

The *Hood* is a most important item in the paraphernalia of a trained Hawk, and one that every Falconer should be able to make for himself. In order to enable him the more readily to do this, we will endeavour to explain the various modes adopted. The Rufter-hood is the most simple description of hood, and is only employed for recently taken wild or

Passage Hawks*; it is intended to remain on the bird for some time, for the purpose of taming it, and of accustoming it to one of the usual construction, and is therefore made of such a form that the Hawk can feed readily with it on, but cannot possibly get it off. It is made without plume, as also without the braces by which the hood proper is opened and closed, and is fastened by a single leathern string which encircles the bottom of it, and is secured behind the bird's head by a button or knot (*vide* Plate XXIII. fig. 1).

The Hood proper in its ordinary form is made either from one, or else from three pieces of leather; for a Peregrine or Goshawk the best leather for the purpose is calf, of the substance of which bridles are made, which may be procured from almost any saddler; for the smaller hawks, pig-skin, such as is used for saddles, is sufficiently firm. When made from one piece of leather,—an excellent method, for the pattern of which we are indebted to Mr. Newcome (*vide* Plate XXII. figs. 1 & 2),—very little difficulty will be experienced; the leather having been cut out by the pattern given, the edges that are to be sewn together should be bevelled off, so as to make a neat seam; and when both sides have been sewn, the whole should be damped by means of a wet sponge or tow, and fashioned into shape on a block of wood, made similar in size to the head of the Hawk† for which the hood is intended, with this exception, that the part corresponding to the eyes of the bird must be *bossed* out, in order that the hood when on may not press upon these important organs. The hood, having been drawn tight upon the block while damp, is secured there by means of a few small tacks and allowed to

---

* In former days it was the practice to *seel* fresh-caught hawks, that is, tie the eyelids together by passing a fine needle and thread through each. This barbarous custom has been entirely given up at home, though still retained in the East.

† A Peregrine Falcon's hood will do equally well for the Goshawk; while that suitable for a female Merlin or Hobby will fit the female Sparrow Hawk.

dry; after this, the lower edge is bound with a strip of thin leather or damped parchment; the plume, by which it is to be held when used, is attached to the top, and the braces or strings which fasten it on to the bird are added. The plume is usually made from hackle or other feathers tied together with a wax-thread; a couple of slits having been made in the leather of the hood, a piece of leather is put through and stitched to the plume, and then a quantity of coloured worsted, or silk, is also drawn through and secured by a few turns of wax-thread, fine wire being then lapped round the whole. The braces are formed from two strips of tough leather, with a button at the broadest end; each of them is passed through three slits cut in the leather at the back of the hood and crossed to the opposite side, so that the button ends open the hood, while the others draw it tight (*vide* Plate XXIII. figs. 3 & 4). The space through which the bill of the bird protrudes may be pared to suit the individual bird for which the hood is intended. In hoods of this construction no cloth or velvet is used to cover the eye-pieces.

The common or Dutch pattern is made from three pieces of leather; one to form the body of the hood, with two other side- or eye-pieces. The lines where the pieces are to be united should be drawn upon the block, and the pattern cut accordingly. An old well-made Dutch hood when taken to pieces is an excellent guide*. The eye-pieces are covered with cloth or velvet, which is pasted on to the leather, and by being made a little larger than the leather itself, the edges are drawn into the seam formed by the sewing, and so held quite secure; the two eye-pieces are sewn to the body inside out, the edges of the leather having been previously bevelled off; and the whole having been then damped, is reversed, fashioned on the block, secured, and left to dry; afterwards the bottom edge is bound with parchment or thin leather, the

* These Dutch hoods may be obtained through Mr. Pells, or any of the members of the Loo Hawking Club.

plume and braces added as previously described, and the space for the beak cut out of the front (*vide* Plate XXIII. fig. 2). When the braces become too slack they should be renewed.

Another form of hood, taken in a great measure from a Syrian pattern, we have tried for some years, and found to answer well, the *only* objection being that it requires a little more skill in its use than that of the ordinary make; in this hood the back part is formed of a curtain of thick soft buckskin, through several slits in which the braces pass. It has the advantage of not being nearly so liable to come open, and also as less likely to injure the plumage at the back of the bird's head than the Dutch mode (*vide* Plate XXIII. fig. 4). Gutta percha we have also tried, by moulding the material in hot water on to the block in one piece, cutting it into shape, and adding the back curtain. A very light and elastic hood was formed, as long as the material retained its proper character; after some months, however, it became exceedingly brittle, and proved worthless on this account.

To hood a Hawk well requires considerable practice, as well as manual dexterity. Falconers differ in their mode of holding the hood during the operation, each one adopting that plan by which he can best accomplish it; all, however, agree in making use of the tassel, either in putting on the hood or taking it off, as also in drawing or undrawing the braces by means of the teeth on one side and the right hand on the other. Hawks should always be hooded on the fist, the leash being well secured *, and every care taken to avoid frightening them. It is a very good plan to give the bird a mouthful or two of meat, and slip on the hood whilst it is in the act of swallowing. If the bird resists the operation, taking it into a dark room will

---

* From not having been properly held, we have known a Hawk escape from a young Falconer with its hood on. This is a most serious accident, for when a Hawk gets away with its hood on, it will fly as long as its strength lasts.

enable the young Falconer to succeed without entering into a struggle with his bird, which he is by all means to avoid.

The *Brail* is sometimes used in training restive Hawks: it is simply a strip of soft leather about half an inch in breadth, tapering towards either end; a slit of about 2 inches long is made down the centre of the strip; through this slit is put the joint of the Hawk's wing, whilst the wing is closed; one end of the leather is brought under the wing and tied to the other end above it; by this means the wing is retained in its natural position, whilst the bird is at the same time prevented from using it.

The *Lure* is employed in training all the Falcons, as, by means of it, they are kept within bounds when on the wing, and also taken down. It may be made of almost any shape; the principal requisites being, that it should be of sufficient weight to prevent a Falcon from carrying it, and at the same time such as will not injure the feet of the bird when striking at it. One very good plan is to cover a wedge-shaped piece of iron, about $1\frac{1}{2}$ lb. in weight, with a thick layer of tow; over this two strong pieces of leather (in a somewhat heart-shaped form) should be strongly sewn round their margins enclosing the weight, the greatest width at the upper part being about 4 or 5 inches. To the body of this lure are attached two sets of strings, by means of which the meat is fastened on, as well as the wings of birds, to render it more attractive. It should have also a strong leathern strap, about 3 feet long, attached to the upper part by means of a swivel; by this strap, which may have a tassel at its end, the lure is swung round the head of the Falconer, or thrown to a distance. Another common form of lure is that of a large horse-shoe, made of heavy wood, with or without a covering of leather, to which also the wings of birds are fastened, as well as the meat. As soon, however, as the young Hawks leave off any inclination to carry their game, a dead pigeon or other bird, with a few feet of string to it, is quite sufficient to take them down with. In flying young Hawks to the lure, care must be taken not to lower their pitch by showing it during the time they are on the mount. The higher a Peregrine rises in the air the more valuable it is likely to become, as it can then command a larger extent of ground, should the game spring at any distance; and at the same time put forth its greatest speed, which it always displays while descending. Very high flyers, however, make wide circles, and should they range to too great a distance, a live pigeon secured to a string by soft leather jesses may be used in the place of the dead lure to recall them.

The Falconer must protect his left hand and arm on which the Hawks sit with a strong buckskin glove, made like a cavalry gauntlet. To all this necessary apparatus should be added a small semicircular tin box or pouch for carrying the meat in for feeding the Hawks, which is strapped round the waist, and a loud-toned whistle, either for recalling the Hawks, or communicating with an assistant at a distance.

In a former part of the chapter we stated, that provided the young Peregrine had been carefully attended to during its period of liberty, fed from the hand, and taught to re-cognize the lure, very little beyond breaking it to the hood would be required in order to prepare it for the field. Sup-posing, however, on the other hand, that such is not the case, and that the newly taken-up bird is perfectly wild and in-tractable, let us now endeavour to point out the mode of overcoming this disposition. At first it will struggle violently upon feeling the restraint of the jesses, and then, finding it cannot escape, sulk; this is the time to take it upon the fist, replacing it gently whenever it bates off, and at the same time stroking it about the breast and legs with a feather. This drilling must be persevered in from morning to night, until it remains more quietly on the glove, or attempts to re-cover its position when off. At feeding-time the hood may be taken off, and the bird allowed to pull at the meat held under its feet; this should be done at first in some darkened place; in a day or two, however, this precaution will not be necessary, as when hungry it will feed readily in the open air; but little food should be given to it at once, and the hood being replaced, an extra mouthful or two may then be added. It may also be allowed to pull occasionally at the pinion or thigh bone of some bird through the hood. As soon as the Hawk will remain steady upon the fist with the hood on, it must be taught to do the same without it, as also quietly to allow this covering to be replaced. During this part of its education much depends upon the manual dexterity of the trainer. The great point with him is to avoid frightening the bird; in case it is very rebellious the brail may be used, or it may be rendered more tractable by drenching it with cold water, and then taking advantage of its wet state to hood and un-hood it frequently; in the latter treatment care must be taken that the bird is thoroughly dry before night. As soon as it has become sufficiently quiet, neither the brail nor the drench-ing will be necessary; it must be, however, kept as much as possible upon the fist, and be occasionally unhooded and allowed to pull at a piece of tough beef, or the stump of a pinion from which very little meat can be got, and when re-hooded a mouthful or two may be added with advantage. The object in using the hood for Hawks is to keep them quiet until the moment for action arrives, as well as to prevent them from bating when birds rise, or taking alarm at the approach of anything to which they are unaccustomed. Sir John Sebright remarks :—

"It may perhaps appear paradoxical to assert that Hawks, by being kept hooded, are brought nearer to their natural habits, but this is undoubtedly the case; for by this treat-ment they are induced to remain at rest when they are not feeding, or in pursuit of game; and such are their habits in a wild state when left undisturbed."

Directly the bird in training will feed readily on the fist, it must be taught to fly to it for the purpose of being fed; it will soon do this, the distance at which the fist is held being daily increased; a small piece of meat should be then thrown on the ground, the bird allowed to go down and eat it, and then be tempted to return to the fist for fresh food. As soon as this *"Jumping to the fist"* is accomplished, the lure must be introduced, well baited with food, and thrown down, at first close to the Falconer, and by degrees to a distance, as the Hawk learns to know and fly to it; while feeding thereon the Falconer should give a few mouthfuls to his bird from the hand, in order to prevent it from attempting to drag off the lure, which at first it is inclined to do. During this early period of its education it will be necessary to secure the young Hawk by a light but strong *creance*; as soon however as it will fly readily to the lure when thrown to a distance, and not leave it at the approach of the Falconer, this precaution may be discontinued. The Falconer is now to swing the lure at some little distance from an assistant on whose fist the Hawk is supposed to be, calling the Hawk at the same time; and when the bird is attracted and flies towards him, the lure must be thrown out so far as to reach the ground before the Hawk can overtake it, otherwise the feet of the bird might be injured by striking it. By increasing the distance daily, it will soon be taught to come to the Falconer from as far as it can see him: and in order to make it " wait on," as it is called, the Falconer must conceal the lure as soon as the Hawk has nearly reached him from a distance. The bird, upon finding itself disappointed, will immediately mount, and make a circle or two in search of the expected food; the lure must now be thrown out, and the young Hawk well rewarded for its behaviour. By doing this repeatedly (keeping back the lure for some time) the Hawk will learn to mount at once from the fist and circle about the Falconer until fed, turning inwards at his voice, or whistle, or at the sight of the lure. Whilst feeding, the Falconer must, as before, walk round and whistle to his bird, or lie down by the side of the lure and assist it to eat.

Falconers make use of different cries by which they call their Hawks; with some it is "Yo-ho-hup, yohup, yohup," others cry "Helover-helaw-helaw-helope." The birds, however, work to their trainer much more by eye than ear, and any sound that causes them to turn their heads inwards answers the purpose. When the game rises there should be some distinct short cry; many Falconers still use the old cry of "Hooha, ha ha ha," which resembles a wild laugh.

When the young Hawk has been thus rendered perfectly obedient to the lure, it should be entered immediately at the quarry at which it is intended to fly. Pigeons being so easily procured are generally the birds first flown at, until the grouse are ready. If a young Hawk takes grouse well, it is pretty sure to take partridges when September comes in. Should it, however, not have been flown at grouse, it must be kept at pigeons until some partridges can be netted.

Whilst the Hawk is "waiting on," one should be thrown out to it in a string; this will be easily taken, and the Hawk must be allowed to eat it : a few similar lessons will be necessary, the string attached to the quarry being on each succeeding occasion shortened, until not any is left. The Eyess is now ready for the field : the Falconer must always remember, however, to have a live partridge in a bag to throw up, should it not succeed in its first flight, young Hawks being very easily discouraged by failure. If used during the early part of the season for grouse, the Eyess should in the first instance only be tried at weak birds.

When the young Hawks begin to kill their game well, they are more liable to be lost than at any other period, and require very careful management. Newly acquired confidence in their own powers causes this disposition to stray, particularly if kept too long upon the wing.

CHAPTER III.

ON THE DAILY MANAGEMENT OF HAWKS.

THE health and condition of his Hawks is the first point, in their general treatment, which the young Falconer has to study, as any want of attention in the matter of these essentials will entail certain disappointment. Glossy plumage, a full clear eye, accompanied by a good appetite, are sure indexes of what is desirable in this respect, and which can only result from constant cleanliness, fresh air, good food, and regular exercise. There are of course occasionally sickly birds, which no amount of care and attention will cause to look well; such are not worth putting into training.

The condition of the birds may be judged by feeling the muscles of the breast and thighs; these ought to be round and firm. As a general rule, the higher condition the young Hawks can be kept in, so as at the same time to ensure obedience, the better. As, however, the disposition of different birds varies, the Falconer must regulate the amount of food each bird requires to bring it into order; some Hawks fly with the greatest determination while in very high condition, whereas others require the stimulus of hunger to make them exert themselves at all; it is always better, however, to lose a few flights by erring on the side of excess, than to bring the bird into too low a state, which both weakens its powers of flight, lessens its spirit, and causes it to hover about the Falconer.

Hawks to be in health should always be kept as much as possible in the open air, and during bad weather under a shed in a sheltered situation. Those Falconers who prefer placing their Hawks at night in a house or mews should

keep it perfectly dark, and remain with the birds sufficiently
long to see that they settle themselves, and do not " bate off "
their blocks or perch. In the morning about seven o'clock
they may be taken out of the mews, and placed upon blocks
in the open air, without their hoods; this is called " *weather-
ing*." The Falconer must be careful at the same time to
notice whether they have *cast*, during the night, or in other
words, thrown up little balls of the feathers, fur, and other
indigestible portions of their previous day's food; as, by the
state of these castings, the health of the bird may be known :
if firm and dry, all is right; when, on the contrary, the ball
is covered with mucus, and mixed up with undigested meat,
it is a sure sign that the Hawk is not well and requires looking to. Hawks will not fly until they have got rid of these
castings. A morsel or two of meat may be given to the Hawk
when first put out in the morning, particularly if it is
intended that it should bathe before flying. All Hawks
require to have the bath offered to them every third or fourth
day throughout the year; in hot weather, however, more frequently, particularly when they show a disposition to go off
in search of water when flown. Young Peregrines and Merlins during the summer months will often bathe daily. Passage Hawks do not at first like to enter a bath, and should
be pegged down by a short creance near some running shallow
water, and left to themselves for a short time. Some Hawks*,
however, never will bathe; we have noticed this in the case of
adult wild-caught Hobbies ; and as these birds are in general
much infested with vermin, it appears probable that even in a
state of liberty the species differs from its neighbours in its
dislike to water.

The bath consists of a shallow vessel similar to the dark
glazed bowls which are used in some parts of England for
holding milk and cream. The sides of a bath must be quite

---

* A male Goshawk in the possession of one of the authors refuses to bathe ;
it was long confined in a cage, probably without water.

smooth and round, otherwise the leash might be entangled and endanger the Hawk's feathers *. Some prefer the bath to be of zinc, with the edges well rounded over; such a bath has the advantage of being light and portable, and not liable to rust, which one made of tin is. A very good bath, however, may be made by merely sawing off the bottom of an old cask or barrel. The bath should be about 8 inches in depth, and about 32 inches in diameter.

Before entering the water, Hawks almost always sip a little of it, though it is certain that they can live without drinking, the juices of the meat being sufficient for them. In the East, however, water is offered to them at night in a cup; sick birds also, particularly when the disease is in the bowels, will drink frequently. Old Falconers appear to have been in the habit of washing their Hawk's-meat repeatedly; which practice Sir Walter Scott alludes to in his scene in the "Abbot," where Adam Woodcock disputes about the merits of washed or unwashed meats for eyesses. When the meat is *not* perfectly fresh, it is doubtless improved by washing; even dipping it into boiling water is an advantage under these circumstances; otherwise nothing appears to be gained by the practice, except that the food is rendered rather less nutritious, and may be so treated when it is necessary to reduce the condition of the Hawk.

Should the Hawk be required to fly during the day on which it bathes, it must be left unhooded for some time to dry and plume itself, and, if a quiet bird, will not require the hood to be put on until it is made ready for the field; noisy or wild Hawks, however, can only be kept quiet by the use of it. The afternoon is the time when Hawks generally fly the best, and in order to have them in good appetite they should be

* All danger arising from the leash of the Hawk becoming entangled about the bath may be obviated by using a bath sunk in the ground up to its edge with a block close to it, to which each bird may be fastened whilst it is bathing, and replaced immediately afterwards upon its own proper stand.

fed lightly on the day previous to their use, somewhat earlier than the hour of flying. After returning home from the field, they should be unhooded, and kept as quiet as possible for the remainder of the day.

If, however, they are not required to fly, they will need exercise to keep them in health and training. This may be given in different ways: thus Goshawks and Sparrow Hawks, after having been carried about for an hour or two, may be placed in a creance* on a gate at some little distance from the Falconer, and made to fly thence to his fist for food. In case the Peregrines have been hard-worked, it will be sufficient to make them spring a few times from the block to the fist; the usual way, however, is to "put them on the wing" to the lure. When Passage Hawks are wild, the safest mode of exercising them is to "call them off" to a pigeon.

About once a week it will be necessary to grease the jesses and leashes of the birds, particularly if they are in the habit of bathing much. Mutton suet is as good as anything for this purpose, though some Falconers mix a little wax and oil with the fat.

Sir John Sebright considers that Hawks feel no attachment to their master, and that, unlike dogs, "hunger is their only inducement to action." It is very true that unless the stomach of the bird is tolerably empty, the owner of it is not in a condition to fly, as is the case previous to the throwing up of the castings; it does not follow, however, as a consequence, that the Hawk does not feel any pleasure in the sport beyond the expectation of a meal; when not sufficiently hungry, a Hawk is particularly liable to "rake away," and amuse itself with an occasional stoop at any bird that may pass, being at that time under but little control.

One of the authors is in possession of an old Tiercel that will readily capture birds which it has no inclination to eat, such

---

* Creances are less apt to entangle when made of "kip leather," with a short piece of cord at the end.

as snipes, thrushes and blackbirds, and which consequently it must take for "the fun of the thing." A female Goshawk also belonging to the same establishment, on one occasion left a rabbit which it had just taken, to secure a second that rose from a tuft of grass close to where the bird was in the act of feeding on the first one; and its whole appearance indicated great excitement and pleasure.

We have known instances where the birds have shown considerable attachment to their trainer. Merlins, in particular, always recognise their master's approach with signs of welcome. A most remarkable instance of this feeling, as evinced by an old Falcon, will be found in Mr. Knox's work entitled 'Game Birds and Wild Fowl, their Friends and their Foes,' page 177.

In severe weather Hawks require more food to preserve them in health than during the summer months. About one-third of a pound of beef is a good meal for a Falcon, and less than that quantity for other Hawks in proportion to the size of the species. As, however, the amount of food each bird will require must be regulated by its behaviour in the field, it is obviously impossible to lay down any certain rule on this point; this, like many other things, must be left to the judgment of the owner. Each Hawk, however, requires a "gorge" every fourth or fifth day, with one day's interval after it before flying again; this is necessary for the health of the bird, and is exactly what it is subject to in a state of nature during wet or windy weather: it should never be omitted, even when it is necessary to keep the bird entirely without food on the day succeeding that of the "gorge," in order to bring it into good working order. Hawks are seldom in *too high* condition, except after "standing to moult." When, however, it is necessary to lower their condition, it must be done by reducing their allowance of food for several days, not by omitting the "gorge." Although fresh beef is perhaps altogether the best food for a Hawk in exercise, it does not answer equally well for one confined to the block (except during the moulting time); a less nourishing diet, such as rabbits, birds, and mice, is to be preferred; and even while in full work, a portion of the game it kills may always be given to the trained Hawk, as much for the sake of its health as to reward it for its performances. Some plumage or fur to produce castings is indispensable, and this is best given in the natural state. Thus, the skin of a crow or pigeon turned inside out with the feathers on, dipped in blood, makes excellent castings; also bruised rabbits' feet dipped in water; even cotton wool mixed with the food will answer the purpose, if feathers or fur are not at hand. The meat is sometimes chopped up into a pulpy state with the addition of a little water and the yolk of a raw egg, and so given to the Hawk: crows and pigeons may be treated in a similar manner, the breast-bone, skin, and intestines having been previously removed. Goshawks are less particular as to their appetite, and will do well on any coarse food, such as rats, squirrels, kittens, &c.

CHAPTER IV.

FIELD MANAGEMENT OF PEREGRINES. — MODE OF CONVEY-
ANCE.—METHOD OF TAKING UP SHY HAWKS.—GAME AND
OTHER FLIGHTS.

BEFORE introducing the young Falconer to the scenes he
may expect to witness in the field from a well-managed
Hawking establishment, it may be as well to allude to the
sort of weather absolutely necessary to the carrying on of this
sport. The more calm and clear the atmosphere is (on the
day selected) the better; during windy weather it is only at
a great risk of loss that Hawks can be flown at any quarry;
although, if under good command, it is an excellent plan to
exercise them, under such circumstances, to the lure: struggling against a strong breeze very much improves their
powers of flight, and affords at the same time a fine display
of the aërial evolutions they are obliged to make in order to
gain headway. Rain, and intense cold, with falling snow, also
very much interfere with the amusement; and even very
hot sunshine is unsuitable *, the Hawks being then inclined
to " take to the soar and rake away," in search apparently of
a cooler current of air at a great elevation; during the prevalence therefore of great heat, it is desirable not to fly the
birds until the cool of the evening. Young Hawks are at
first very shy about coming down to the lure when thrown
on the ground covered with snow; this fear, however, they

---

* About midday in India, when the heat is insupportable, the birds of prey
ascend out of sight. On a very hot day in England, a young Tiercel belonging to
a friend of ours "took to the soar," and remained an hour and twenty minutes out
of sight. We have also known Hawks soar just after the breaking up of a long
frost; this, in the early spring, may perhaps be attributed to a desire to join a mate,
which induces even Sparrow Hawks in their wild state to mount to a great height.

soon overcome, and great sport may be sometimes had over a
snow-clad country.   As it may be fairly said that no other
description of field sports is so much influenced by the state
of the weather, in making Hawking appointments, there
should always be a proviso on this point.

If only a couple of Hawks are taken to the field, these may
be easily carried on the arm; but a greater number require
the "cadge *," either of the usual form, as shown in Plate V.;
or, where the distance is considerable, and the mode of conveyance is railway or carriage, by placing them upon the "spring
box cadge," which is simply an oblong box without a lid,
sufficiently large for the purpose, having broad padded edges
for the hawks to sit upon, and supporting springs attached
to the bottom for the purpose of lessening the jar, holes
being made in the sides immediately below the padded rim
for passing the leashes through.   Some birds, particularly
Passage Hawks, require the brail, or a wetting, to make them
sit quiet while on the cadge; in general, however, this restraint is not necessary.

In addition to his birds, the Falconer will require in the
field two or three live pigeons for lures, easily carried in a
fishing-creel, or in a circular bag, kept open by having a stiff
leather bottom, and a cane hoop or two of the same diameter
sewn inside half-way up; with a leather bag for carrying the
iron pins to which the Hawks are secured on the ground, similar to those by which they are fastened at their blocks, as well
as spare hoods and leashes. An opera-glass is also of great use
in looking for missing birds, or for watching a distant flight;
and in case any of the young Hawks are too shy to be readily
approached and taken up, the Falconer should be provided
with some small cord for the purpose of snaring them; this

---

* The "cadge" is a light wooden framework on which several Hawks can be
carried by one man; it is made either oblong or circular, with space in the centre
for the Falconer, to whose shoulders it is slung by means of straps. The Hawks
are fastened to it in the same manner as to the "screen."

is effected while the bird is in the act of feeding either on the quarry it may have taken, or upon some lure thrown to it for the purpose, by fastening one end of the cord to a peg at some little distance from the Hawk, or by employing an assistant to hold the end, and then, by walking * three or four times round it, carrying the line, and cautiously twisting it round its legs above the bell, and so securing it. Another mode is to peg down a pigeon, which it has been previously allowed to kill, with a noose arranged around it, a few of the pigeon's wing-feathers having been stuck obliquely into the ground, just within the noose sloping upwards and inwards, so as to guide the string when pulled up the Hawk's legs. If a Hawk has been lost † for some time, it may be taken (provided it is hungry) in the *Bow Net* with a live pigeon.

Should the Hawk appear very shy, it will probably clutch the pigeon after repeated stoops, when it will fly off with its victim. The Falconer must allow it to carry the bird a short distance, and then bring it to the ground by quietly pulling the line, and whilst the Hawk's attention is fully occupied with the struggling pigeon he must lose no time in drawing both gently within the net, until they come up to the eye of the pin in the centre, when he must instantly pull the other half of the net over them (*vide* Plate XXIV. fig. 3, as also the capture of Passage Hawks, Chap. V.).

Some Falconers are expert at a third method of snaring a shy Hawk that will only clutch up the pigeon as it flies past, and as a snare has the advantage over the bow net by its being

---

* In walking round a shy Hawk always keep moving, and apparently not taking notice of it. In order to catch a Hawk that has been long at large and is very shy, throw it a live pigeon in a string and walk off from it; if it takes it and begins to eat, go up and frighten it off, and then set your snare or bow net and retire until it comes down to eat again, when you may be sure of it.

† A lost Hawk is often pointed out by the croaking of Carrion Crows, and the commotion its appearance makes amongst Rooks, Magpies, &c. A Goshawk may often be found amongst trees by the chirp of the Chaffinch before the bell is heard.

more rapidly set and always at hand: we shall here explain how it is done. Peg down a dead pigeon, and place a slip-knot round it so as to entangle the Hawk's feet when it strikes; this noose should be fastened to something that will merely impede the bird's flight sufficiently to render its capture easy, otherwise its legs might be dislocated by the sudden jerk.

A small pair of *clap-nets*, made of silk or fine twine, of a large mesh, render the capture of even a wild Hawk almost certain, as they will take the bird either while merely passing over the lure, or upon its alighting within their sweep. A long pull line should be used with these nets, and the person employed should conceal himself.

The " Falconer's bag * " of our ancestors, and which we often see represented in the paintings of Wouvermans and others, is but little used at the present day, at least in this country; it was a large bag with several divisions in it, having a metal rim, sometimes highly ornamented, and fastened to the waist by a swivel-hook. A small light one or tin box for carrying the Hawk's meat is, however, a useful addition to the Falconer's apparatus.

We are now supposed to have reached open ground, and will commence with a description of Pigeon Hawking. These birds, from being so readily obtained, are the quarry at which young Peregrines are usually *entered*; and when those only are used which are strong and lately caught, are as fully equal to test the speed and "*footing qualities*" of the best Hawks as any denizen of the wilds; for, although commonly

---

* In Dr. Whitaker's ' History of Craven,' page 180, there is an engraving of a rim to a very ancient " Falconer's bag;" this rim is of brass, with the angelical salutation in Latin engraved upon it; it was found near Gargrave, on the site of a mansion belonging to a family of that name. Another very beautiful perfect bag with its case, of Elizabethan date, in the possession of Mr. Fitch of Norwich, is composed of green velvet, ornamented with gold embroidery, and tassels, having also gold bells, and a swivel hook of the same precious metal; on one side are several texts of Scripture, and other lines; the case is made of wood covered with green silk.

called domestic birds, it is only from the circumstance of their breeding under the protection of man that they can be so classed; they range over the whole country in search of food, and pass more time on the wing than any other species of grain-eating birds, and although not so strong, are far more swift than the cushat or wild ring-dove. For this flight either Falcon or Tiercel may be used, singly, or a cast of either sex when they will work peaceably together. Two Tiercels give perhaps the best sport, for as the flight with a good blue rock pigeon will probably last for some minutes, and may extend to a couple of miles, the two Hawks, like greyhounds, will both endeavour to outvie each other, as well as to capture their prey, each one taking up the stroke which its neighbour has just missed. A country as devoid as possible of trees or hedges should be selected for this sport. The pigeon in general tries, in the first instance, the powers of its pursuers both up and down wind, and sometimes "takes the air" fairly, or endeavours to mount above them; failing in these attempts, which however is by no means always the case, it will either be struck and taken, or it will seek shelter in the first bush it can reach, and there the sport terminates; for upon feeling its inferiority in the air it will make no further efforts, but endeavour only to conceal itself. The Hawks should be high up before the pigeon is turned off, and "good law" should be given the latter, for although it shifts to avoid the stroke with great rapidity, the first stoop is the most difficult to escape from.

Falconers encourage or call the attention of their Hawks upon the springing of the quarry by some distinct cry; the usual one being "Hooha-ha-ha-ha-ha!" (as before mentioned). Upon killing, the cry is "Whoop!" and that to give notice to the field upon viewing a lost Hawk is "Up-ho!"

The wild pigeon or cushat, in summer, is seldom found sufficiently far from cover to make a successful flight. During the winter, however, especially if there is much snow on the ground, these birds congregate and frequent turnip fields, often at a considerable distance from their usual retreats; under such circumstances we have had very good sport: they are not nearly so swift as the common dove-cot pigeon, and a Hawk will come up with them from a great distance; they, however, shift well to avoid the stroke, but are altogether, on open ground, an easier bird to kill than their domestic congener. Woodcocks, when found upon the open country, as in the little dingles and patches of birch wood on the moor edges, show splendid sport. The Hawk for this flight should be a high flier; and when beating a hill side, it is a great advantage if the wind blows against it, as, when this is the case, the Hawk mounts into the current of air which rises above the hill, and is thus easily suspended over the Falconer's head, where it "hangs on," at a great pitch, ready for the quarry. Before putting the Hawk upon the wing, a woodcock * should be flushed by the beaters or dogs, and marked down; upon this being done, the Hawk is thrown off, and time must be given it, in order that it may mount to a good height before the game is again sprung; should the woodcock "take the air" (as it is termed), a fine struggle for superiority in that element may be looked for; often, however, it makes for the nearest cover.

The best sport shown by John Anderson was at woodcocks. He was accustomed to come over from Barocan Tower with his birds, and stay at Kelly, the seat of the late Robert Wallace, Esq., in Renfrewshire. The plantations there were at that time too young to interfere with the sport; and it was from Kelly Glen, &c., that he had some of his finest flights. On one occasion General Sir Maxwell Wallace witnessed so beautiful a flight, that we shall endeavour to describe it as it was told by him to one of the authors. A woodcock was flushed on a rough braeside, and having been marked down

* Hawks that have been flown much at snipes in the earlier part of the season, make the best birds for woodcocks.

in the open, a favourite Tiercel was flown, and allowed to attain a commanding position ; upon the woodcock being again sprung, it made a rapid zigzag flight over the broad mouth of the Clyde, but finding it could not gain the opposite shore in safety, it returned for the country it had left. The Tiercel pursued it eagerly, making the most beautiful stoops, which the quarry as adroitly evaded, until within two or three hundred yards of the shore, when a fatal stroke brought it dead upon the water. The spaniels, seeing this, dashed in, and one of them brought the woodcock in triumph to land, attended by the Tiercel " waiting on " above its head. The Scotch Falconer, having taken up the bird, which had been deposited at his feet, threw it to his well-trained Hawk to " take his pleasure on," whilst the spaniels bayed around with delight ; all who witnessed the scene declaring it worthy to be immortalized on canvass.

When Francis M'Cullock was Falconer to John Sinclair *, Esq., of the Falls, near Belfast, his master had a wonderful Falcon for taking woodcocks †. With this famous bird Mr. Sinclair visited the Hon. R. Westenra at Rossmore Park, in the county of Monaghan, Ireland, and while there Mr. Sinclair had a most extraordinary flight with this Hawk. Mr. Knox, in his work ' Game Birds and Wild Fowl, their Friends and their Foes,' page 171, gives a most interesting description of this scene, which we will quote for the benefit of our readers. " When Mr. Sinclair and his Falconer M'Cullock (afterwards Falconer to Colonel Bonham) were hawking woodcocks in Rossmore Park, a woodcock was flushed, which ' took the air,' closely pursued by the Falcon, which had Mr. Sinclair's address upon the varvels. In a short time both Hawk and quarry had attained such an elevation, that it was only by lying down on their backs, and placing their hands above their eyes, so as to screen them from the rays of the sun, and

* He was in this gentleman's service from 1823 to 1833.
† She took fifty-seven in one season.

at the same time contract the field of vision, that the spectators could keep the birds within view. At last, just as they had become mere specks in the sky, they were observed to pass rapidly towards the north-east, under the influence of a strong south-west wind, and were soon entirely out of sight. Some days elapsed without any tidings of the truant Falcon; but, before the week had expired, Mr. Sinclair received a letter (forwarded from his home) bearing a Scottish post-mark. The letter contained the varvels, and the closing chapter of the poor Hawk's history, from the hand of her destroyer, a farmer who resided within ten miles of Aberdeen. He was walking through his grounds, when his attention was attracted by the appearance of a large Hawk, which had just dashed amongst his pigeons, and was then in the act of carrying off one of them; running into the house, he returned presently with a loaded gun, and found the robber devouring her prey on the top of a wheat stack; the next moment the unfortunate Falcon's wanderings were at an end: but it was not until he had seen the bells on her feet, that he discovered the value of his victim, and upon a more careful examination perceived the name and address of her owner; and whilst making him the only reparation in his power, by sending the account of her fate, he unconsciously rendered the story worthy of record in a sporting as well as ornithological point of view; for upon a subsequent comparison of dates, it was found that the bird had been shot near Aberdeen, on the eastern coast of Scotland, within forty-eight hours after she had been flown at a woodcock in a central part of the province of Ulster in Ireland!"

For snipe-hawking Tiercels are generally preferred; and good sport may be had with this quarry during the early part of the season, as the old birds, at that time going through the moult, are within the powers of the *young* Hawks; after that period it is but seldom that a "snipe*" that "rings" or

---

* Colonel Thornton, in his 'Northern Tour,' describes a ringing snipe flight which lasted nine minutes.

"takes the air" is killed, unless cut down by the first lucky stoop from a clever Hawk. We have seen them, however, repeatedly beaten down by a favourite Tiercel after the snow has been for some days on the ground, when they would take shelter under a snow wreath, or in any cover they could reach; probably, under such circumstances, the difficulty of procuring food had diminished their powers of flight. Hawks used for this quarry should be quite free from the fault of "carrying."

Game hawking comprehends grouse, black game, partridges and pheasants; the first-mentioned species affords by far the highest sport, and tests the powers of the best Hawks most severely. Old grouse fly down wind with great rapidity, and, owing to the dark colour of the ling, close to which they keep when pursued by the Hawk, there is considerable difficulty in marking them to any distance. This fact, combined with the usually uneven nature of the ground on which they are found, renders the sport more hazardous, as far as the loss of the Hawk is concerned, than perhaps any other description of hawking. To obviate this danger as much as possible, some of the company present should be mounted, and must make every endeavour to keep the birds during the flight within sight. An old cock grouse will probably lead even a fast Hawk a mile away from the spot on which it sprung.

A good high-ranging pointer or setter, which should, of course, be well acquainted with the Hawks, and work *to* them, is requisite for this sport *. As soon as the dog points, the Hawk should be unhooded and thrown off; this prevents the game from rising; and when the bird has attained a good pitch (the higher the better), and is nearly overhead, the grouse may be flushed; should it prove an old bird, and evade the first stoop, which is always by far the most deadly, a fair trial

---

* Dogs that have been much used with Hawks appear to be quite aware of the position the bird ought to be in, and will either keep back or spring the game as the Hawk is well or badly placed.

of speed (down wind) will commence. When the ground
rises, and the game turns its head upwards, this will prove
greatly in favour of the quarry, a Falcon always showing to
advantage while descending, and losing way in flying up-hill.
Where the moor is very rough, the grouse, if sufficiently
ahead of the Hawk, will seek cover; but upon bare ground
it will make every exertion to maintain its position by strength
of wing, and will probably fall a victim to its enemy's
greater powers of endurance.

It is necessary to keep even Falcons* in constant practice
at grouse hawking to ensure success throughout the season.
Late in September, and during the following month, when
the grouse come down in packs on to the stubbles, Hawks
that have been accustomed to fly them on the moors, show
excellent sport. By watching the arrival of the grouse,
and then by getting between them and the ground whence
they came, and throwing off a Hawk, the Falconer may walk
into the midst of the pack crouching on the ground, and with
his bird at a good pitch overhead, will have every chance of a
killing flight on the open stubble. The sooner Hawks are
entered at this quarry the better, even though it should be

---

* Though Tiercels are sometimes used for grouse hawking, very few have
sufficient courage to take them. Certain it is that they do not want strength,
for some of the very best grouse Hawks,—Hawks that could take grouse the whole
season through,—have been Tiercels, such as Mr. Barr's "Wee Pet," and some
old Tiercels of John Anderson's, who always preferred a good high-mounting
old Tiercel to a Falcon. The country this Falconer liked best was an extensive
moss, with but few grouse upon it, that the Hawk might not be led off from one
to another. He chose a moss, because such places are of course always perfectly
flat and open. Being sure of finding, he cast off the Tiercel and allowed it to
get to its pitch, and then, with a good high-ranging pointer, well-accustomed to
grouse and to hawks, he soon had a point. When the dog stood, the Hawk
(knowing what this meant) came right above him, and upon flushing the quarry
the Tiercel was almost certain to have one at the first stoop, and Anderson a
brace with his unerring gun. The old Hawk having been rewarded, was again
flown for two or three times with generally equal success, and at each flight he
mounted higher and higher.

necessary to anticipate the dates a little : killing a few young birds has a wonderful effect in encouraging the Hawks to exert themselves subsequently at stronger game *.

If the Hawk kills, the Falconer alone should attempt to approach it ; this he must do very carefully, especially if the bird shows any signs of impatience ; and by allowing it to commence eating its prey before he attempts to secure it, he will not have much difficulty in slipping the leash through the slits at the ends of the jesses. If a young Hawk, and if this is the *first bird* it has killed, it will be as well to peg it down where it is, and allow it to plume and gorge upon it ; but if it has killed before, it may eat the head, and have a morsel of beef given to it from the hand. This is the most effectual mode of preventing any disposition to " carry," which Hawks evince, not from their natural wildness, but from the fear of being deprived of their meal. It may be then taken up with the dead quarry, and either fed immediately, or hooded, and retained for another flight.

Black game, while young, are easily killed by Falcons, and even Tiercels have been tried with success. With an old black cock, however, it is a different matter, and only a very high-couraged and powerful Falcon is equal to the attempt. These birds do not fly with much speed, and the Hawks easily come up with them ; but they are very strong and difficult to secure when brought down.

Partridge hawking may be practised wherever the country is sufficiently open, and the enclosures large. A good setter or pointer, together with a couple of spaniels (Clumber breed) well under command, are necessary for carrying out the sport well. As soon as the former has found birds, the Hawk should be cast off, and allowed to get to a high pitch ; for as the

---

* All Hawks pursue with the greatest eagerness that species of game at which they are *constantly* flown. We have seen Hawks in Norfolk so well broken to rooks, that they would not notice partridges, which abounded there. To the same end Game-Hawks ought not to be flown at rooks or pigeons.

flight is always in a straight line, the only fine part consists
in the impetuous rush of the Hawk from a great elevation.
When the covey rises, the Hawk selects one bird, and dashes
down (sometimes passing through the others) in pursuit, and
either strikes it down*, or drives it into the shelter of a fence;
in the latter case the Hawk rises in the air immediately above
the spot where the partridge has taken refuge : this is called
" making its point." The Falconer now loses no time in
coming with the spaniels to the assistance of his bird, and
whilst it is "waiting on" overhead, he again springs the quarry
thus " put in :" this may be repeated more than once. Should,
however, there be a difficulty in recovering the hunted partridge, a live one from the Falconer's bag should be thrown
up to the young Hawk as a reward for its exertions. As an
old partridge only weighs about a pound, young Falcons can
easily carry one; every care must therefore be taken to prevent the Hawk doing so. Late in the season, when the birds
become wild, and the country is sufficiently open, Sir John
Sebright recommends the sport to be carried on by the party
galloping in a line fifty or sixty yards apart, with the Falconer in the centre, and slightly in advance, who regulates
the pace, and keeps his Hawk "waiting on" at a high pitch.
He speaks of having seen in this way the best sport partridges afford. Sometimes also, with very wild game, the
Hawk is flown at them " *out of the hood*," that is, unhooded,
and thrown off the moment the birds rise : in this case the
partridges are almost certain to gain some cover before the
Hawk can come up with them; but being thus " put in,"
the Hawk has time to get to its pitch, and upon the birds
being again flushed, a proper flight may be obtained. A cast
of Hawks which have been accustomed to work together, and
will not fight, may be used in partridge hawking, as when
the covey rises, they will probably select different birds, and
render the flight more interesting ;—a safe precaution, under

---

* We have known a Tiercel cut off the head of a partridge at the first stoop.

all circumstances, is to have markers posted on some rising ground down wind, and near to any cover.

Falconers generally consider that three flights during one day are sufficient for a Peregrine. Many good birds, however, can do more work than this with success. For instance, an Eyess Falcon called " Jenny Lind," the property of the Falconer William Barr, killed in one day six partridges, near Warminster in Wilts, in 1850. We have been kindly favoured by the Duke of Leeds with a list of game killed by his Grace's Hawks, when, as Marquis of Carmarthen, he lived at Dunottar House, near Stonehaven, Kincardineshire :—

" Diamond," a Falcon, killed in 1830,

Grouse	15
Partridges	65
Woodcock	1
	81 head.

" Pearl," a Falcon, killed in 1830,

Grouse	15
Partridges	63
Woodcock	1
Rooks	2
	81 head.

" Macduff," a Tiercel, killed in 1830,

Grouse	4
Partridges	68
Woodcocks	3
	75 head.

" The General," a Tiercel, killed in 1830,

Grouse	11
Partridges	64
Woodcocks	3
Landrail	1
Magpie	1
	80 head.

In 1832 this excellent Tiercel killed,

Partridges	123
Woodcocks	6
	129 head out of 134 flights !

We can also mention the performances of two other first-rate Tiercels, though we regret that a regular list of what they killed has not been kept.

During the year 1845, Mr. Barr * brought up an Eyess Tiercel, which from its great docility and excellence he called " *Wee Pet* †." This wonderful Hawk flew so much " at hack,"

* The father of William Barr the Falconer.

† This bird so well understood the assistance it derived from the dogs, that it would stoop at them while pointing (as if to urge them on to spring the game) and immediately regain its pitch.

that it might be almost said to have lived at large : it would follow its master to the hills, " waiting on " at a high pitch for a couple of hours at a time, and would always return home, if not taken down.   It killed grouse, partridges, grey hens, cock and hen pheasants, pewits, snipes, larks and Royston crows, and died in its fifth year, from the effects of swallowing a stone about the size of a horse-bean.

In 1850 William Barr brought up a Tiercel which proved a very superior Hawk : it was called " Bishop," after the well-known sporting dignitary of Bond Street.   This Tiercel (now the property of one of the authors) has a short strong body, with remarkably rakish wings, which accounts for its great speed.   It has killed grouse, partridges (both the grey- and red-legged), ptarmigans, grey hens and young black cocks, a teal, a cock pheasant, woodcocks, snipes, pewits, blackbirds, thrushes, fieldfares, starlings, stonechats, titlarks, magpies, and house pigeons beyond number.

Flying Hawks repeatedly over the same country does not appear to have the effect of banishing the game from the ground, as is often supposed ; the same covey of partridges may be found day after day, all through the season, almost in the same spot, and if not subjected to the persecution of " vile saltpetre," will afford many an exciting moment to man, beast and bird.

Pheasants may be killed with Falcons when they stray sufficiently far from cover to offer the chances of a fair flight ; for this game, however, the Goshawk is better suited (particularly the male), either in or out of cover.

Magpie Hawking in a good country affords great amusement, from the extreme sagacity displayed by the quarry in its efforts to escape, requiring in consequence the active assistance of all present in order to effect its capture.   An open common with occasional bushes is the best ground for the sport.   The instant a magpie is seen, a Tiercel should be unhooded and thrown off (the braces of the hood having been previously slackened, in order that the favourable moment should not be lost) ; the magpie immediately seeks the shelter of the nearest bush, where it remains concealed until driven out by the cracking of the whips of the assistants : while passing to a second bush, the Hawk, if in position, may be enabled to make his stoop ; this the magpie will avoid with great adroitness, taking advantage of every inequality in the ground that may aid him, even passing occasionally under the horses of the riders, and always endeavouring to make for some strong cover ; it must be the object of his pursuers to prevent this, by driving him as much as possible into the open ground. A second Hawk may now be cast off ; but even with this additional assistance it will be long before his resources fail him, and exhaustion alone will compel him to succumb. This sport has some analogy to fox-hunting, where both the objects of pursuit are themselves robbers, and at the same time fully equal to the emergency of their position. As this quarry in a good suitable country gives so much sport, of course Falconers preserve them with as much jealousy as other sportsmen do the fox.

We now come to a somewhat similar sport, viz. *Rook hawking* ; this is perhaps the very best quarry at which Falcons can in general be flown, to be met with everywhere, particularly on open downs otherwise almost destitute of game, and with no mean powers of wing : the rook, the carrion crow, and the Royston crow are favourite objects of pursuit *. It was at one time imagined that only Passage Hawks were equal to this quarry ; Sir John Sebright, however, proved the contrary to be the fact, and it is now admitted by all Falconers, that Eyesses, which have flown long at hack, are

* Colonel Thornton used to tether a cat under a *dead tree*, which had the effect of luring up crows, by which means he often got excellent flights in a country which he selected ; for the tree was not one that had grown there, but a small dead tree which he put down and removed at pleasure. We find that a Goshawk placed out in the same way will bring up crows from any distance.

in all respects equally good for the purpose: Sir John considers a cast of Falcons requisite. We have, however, seen a single bird take rooks admirably, and even Tiercels are occasionally met with possessing sufficient courage and strength for rook flying.

Mr. Barr has taken rooks with Eyess Tiercels, as also has his son William; indeed one of William Barr's best rook Hawks in 1852 was an eyess Tiercel, with which, upon first "entering" it, he took seven rooks out of nine flights. One of the authors had an eyess Tiercel, which, while at hack, and for some time afterwards, flew rooks readily. Mr. Newcome in 1838 had a Tiercel called "Will-o'-the-Wisp," which proved a first-rate rook Hawk; this bird was, however, a Passage Hawk; it died in its fifth year. Mr. O'Keef used Eyess Falcons for rooks, and flew but one at a time; and in the course of three weeks he killed upon the Curragh of Kildare 117, having upon one occasion as many as fifty-seven turns with one rook.

A very open country destitute of trees is required for this sport; the very best ground being the South Downs, such as the country about Lavington near Devizes, East Ilsley in Berkshire, and Warminster in Wiltshire, &c.

Hawks intended for rooks should, during the time they are thus employed, be flown at no other quarry; on entering them it is necessary to give them two or three of the birds from the hand, and their early flights should be if possible at young rooks. In seeking for this quarry it is always a great object to meet with them as far as possible down wind of their breeding ground, so that the birds in order to reach their home must fly against the wind. The best month for the sport is during a *dry* March, when the old cock birds wander far in search of food for their mates, and when the Eyesses of the preceding season are still in good plumage and have had several months' work. Some of the company should be mounted for this sport, and endeavour by cracking their

whips to keep the quarry upon the wing. Rooks will sometimes fairly take the air, but in general their efforts are to
escape to cover. While speaking of these birds we may mention a curious scene witnessed by one of the authors, showing
very strongly the predatory habits of the carrion crow: it
was during a flight at a house pigeon with a single Tiercel
that a corbie joined in the pursuit; not in any way attempting
to interfere with the Hawk, but in fact proving itself a valuable assistant; for, upon the pigeon taking refuge in a tree,
the crow immediately followed, and put it out to the Tiercel
"waiting on" above; this was repeated several times, and
ended in the death of the quarry; the crow, upon the termination of the sport, contenting itself with watching the proceed-
ings of the Hawk from the top of a neighbouring tree. Leaving
the birds in this position, the owner went for another pigeon
and a second Hawk; upon his return to the spot, the crow
had been joined by a companion, and both of them appeared
deeply interested in the meal which the more fortunate
Tiercel had commenced. Upon taking up this Hawk, and
then casting it off again together with the second, and giving
the fresh pigeon good "law," a most interesting flight commenced, all four birds joining in it; the crows endeavouring
to make up for their deficiency of speed by cutting off the
angles whenever an opportunity occurred. After a long
struggle, in which the quarry, which "took the air," seemed
likely to have the best of it, it lost its advantage by attempting to dart down from a considerable height into a clump of
trees; in this the Hawks were more than its equal, and took
it at the moment of its entering the cover: as before, the
crows perched themselves on a neighbouring tree, and doubtless expected to come in for the remains of the feast. Jack-
daws may be flown in precisely the same way as rooks, but
being more active birds, are not very easily killed.

Wild ducks and teal, when met with in small pools on the
moors, or in brooks, so that they can be driven from the

water, give very good sport. Eyess Falcons are almost certain to fly them readily. Colonel Thornton, however, mentions that the only Tiercels he could meet with equal to this flight were from *one* eyrie on the Hamilton Hills, near Goremire, which now no longer exists. In North America and in Ireland the Peregrine is called the *Duck Hawk*, from its propensity to prey upon this quarry. In this sport the Hawk may be either flown from the air, or " out of the hood; " the former is the better mode, where the duck can be easily forced to rise. The crack of a whip is almost certain to put it up, even with the Hawk overhead: if there is any wind at the time, the duck will fly with great rapidity down it, and lead the Hawk a good chase; when hard-pressed it will endeavour to make for some water, and if possible to dash in from under the Hawk when the latter makes its stoop. When the Hawk is flown from " out of the hood," the duck will get a good start and probably " take the air."

The curlew, and Norfolk or thick-kneed plover are sometimes flown with Peregrines; in fact, the former of these two birds is a very difficult quarry to capture. Passage Hawks which have been accustomed to fly herons are the best for the purpose; it is necessary to ride to these birds, which often go a long distance. The Norfolk plover seldom takes the air, and makes an easy flight.

CHAPTER V.

ON THE CAPTURE AND TRAINING OF PASSAGE HAWKS.—
HERON HAWKING.

THE term Passage Hawk is always applied, *par excellence*, by Falconers to the migrating Peregrine, although other Hawks, under similar circumstances, might come under the same denomination. These birds of prey appear to follow that law of instinct which to a greater or less degree influences nearly the whole of the feathered tribe*, and induces them, at the approach of winter, to leave the neighbourhood of their breeding grounds, and either to congregate in numbers in some particular localities, or, as is more generally the case, to travel far towards the south, and pass the dreary winter months under a more favoured climate. Among the species in which we are more particularly interested, the Hobby is only a summer visitant amongst us, always retreating periodically towards the south. The Merlin leaves, in a great measure, the moors throughout the northern part of the island, and is at that time constantly killed in the southern counties. The Sparrow Hawk in this country evidently shifts its ground, being taken in the bird-catcher's nets far more frequently during the *flight season* in October and November than at any other time; whilst at Malta and other islands in the Mediterranean it is caught in great numbers migrating from Europe towards Africa. Lastly, the Peregrine seeks for winter quarters in the same direction; and on its

---

* Perhaps with some species a scarcity of food for *all* may be one cause of this migration; for certain it is that some remain all the winter with us, and perhaps these are the oldest and strongest birds, which probably drive off the younger and weaker ones.

way from the eyries of this country *, and probably from Norway and Sweden, passes over the extensive heaths in Valkenswaard in Holland, where from time immemorial it has been the business of the inhabitants to capture and train this bird in the mode we are now about to describe.

A small hut, which conceals the Hawk-catcher, is formed by digging a hole of the diameter required, and then constructing a low wall, raised but little above the surface of the ground with the removed turf, and covering the whole with a roof, of which the wooden framework is usually an old cartwheel, the whole being covered with turf, and rendered as little conspicuous as possible. In this hut the man has the cords attached to the "*bow-net*," and to the live pigeons, which he is thus able to work (by their passing through holes in the hut door) without being himself visible.

Before we proceed further, it will be necessary to describe the bow-net. This is a circular net of fine twine, and is made to bag sufficiently in the centre so as not to press upon the captured Hawk. It is fastened to a round frame, made by bending two iron bars (five-sixteenths in size) into semicircles and joining them by loops at their ends which act as hinges. When put together and laid out flat, this framework should measure 3 feet 4 inches from hinge to hinge, and 4 feet 10 inches across the other way. When set, only half the net is allowed to move, viz. that half to which the pull-line is to be attached; the other half is firmly pegged to the ground by means of three *square*-headed pegs, which hold better than when round-headed. The net is set by turning back the moveable bow and pull-line, and after adjusting the net and covering the whole with either soil or pulled grass or moss, it is baited with a pigeon (*vide* Plate XXIV. fig. 3).

At a moderate distance from the hut the bow-net is fixed, and beyond it a small box, with a moveable door, containing

---

* The Hawk-catchers in Holland have on several occasions taken Hawks that have escaped from Norfolk.

a live pigeon fastened to a string leading from the hut: this pigeon, at the approach of a Hawk, can be drawn out of the box into the centre of the net by means of the string, which passes through a ring-headed pin fixed there. Nearer to the hut a tall pole is set up, to which is fastened another live pigeon of a light colour, by means of braces round the body, having a small swivel on the back of the bird, with a string sufficiently long to allow it to seek shelter under a small sod set up for the purpose. In addition to this, the Hawk-catcher employs a butcher-bird to give him warning when a Hawk is in sight; this it does by uttering loud cries and taking refuge under a similar sod, as soon as it perceives the enemy. The Hawk-catcher makes one pigeon fly up, by pulling the string attached to the pole, and so lures up the Hawk. Directly the Passage Hawk sees this pigeon, she dashes at it; it creeps under the sod; and whilst the disappointed bird is circling about, the second pigeon is drawn out of the box into the centre of the bow-net, where it is seized by the Hawk; upon this the catcher draws the cord or wire of his net, which flies up through the light earth which has concealed it, and encircles the struggling birds. The prize is secured as quickly as possible, a "rufter hood" is put on, and the bird itself is secured in a sock *, until such time as the catcher can reach home. As soon, however, as he does this, the fresh-caught Hawk is supplied with jesses, leash, &c., and fastened down to a sod hillock (*vide* Plate VI.). The bird, having only the length of its jesses allowed it, and everything about it being made round

* The sock is merely the ankle part of a cotton stocking drawn over the head of the hooded Hawk, and fastened round its neck, with small slits on each side, through which the joints of the wings pass for about an inch and a half. A couple of waxed strings, secured about 4 inches apart to the sock, are brought round the body of the bird, and then tied. The legs and feet having been put through a hole in the sock, are also secured, by wrapping them up in a cloth. The bird in this mummy state is fastened down to the bottom of a box or basket, on a little hay or straw.

and soft, cannot easily injure itself during its struggles. In this way it is kept for the first week or two, until its regular training commences.

The beak and talons of a fresh-caught Hawk are to be "coped," or in other words, have their points taken off. In many respects the training of a "Haggard*" is precisely similar to that we have already described when speaking of Eyesses; but as the bird has hitherto looked upon man only as a dreaded enemy, and avoided his presence as much as possible, there will be the additional difficulty of overcoming this fear, and replacing the feeling with that of confidence. In order to effect this, the greatest care is required not to startle the bird, or in any way handle it roughly: it must be constantly on the Falconer's fist during the day—at first even for a portion of the night—as want of rest has considerable effect in breaking down the natural wildness of its disposition: a very little food at a time should be given to it by candle-light, the hood having been taken off for the time: for the first day or two probably it will not eat on the fist; should there be any danger, however, of the bird starving †, it must be crammed. As soon as it has become sufficiently tractable to "*pull upon a pinion*" on the fist by daylight, it must be "*made to the hood;*" and as some Hawks resist this operation violently, it should be always practised before the bird has been fed, bating upon a full crop being highly injurious to them: it is, however, a good plan to allow it to pull at a tough piece of beef, or a pinion, through the hood immediately upon its being put on: the feeding-up must be deferred until the evening, after which the bird is left unhooded, but in a darkened place, for the night. Passage Hawks are usually kept

* A Peregrine Falcon is termed " Haggard " when it is taken wild in the adult plumage; during the first year it is called a " Soar Hawk," or a " Red Hawk."

† Hawks that have been kept *too long* without food, lose all power of digestion; it is therefore necessary to give the stomach something to act upon at short intervals.

in a darkened place upon the perch; but some prefer to place them on blocks upon soft grass, or with plenty of straw around them when in the mews. Passage Hawks are trained to the lure, but as they will not wait on, like Eyesses, until they have been two or three years under the Falconer's care, it is considered sufficient if they fly to it when thrown to a distance. They are "taken down," after unsuccessful flights, with a live pigeon in a string.

When the Passage Hawk has become sufficiently tractable to be trusted at large, a live pigeon should be given to it at the block; if it kills this eagerly, on the following day, when sharp set, it may be "put upon the wing," and "called off" at a pigeon in a string, which it must be allowed to kill, and feed upon to the amount of three parts of a crop full. This may be repeated for two or three successive days; after that, it may be allowed a "gorge." The day following the gorge it should not have any food, a small quantity only on the second day, and on the third it will be in order to be trusted to fly an handicapped pigeon—that is, one with the flight feathers shortened.

These, as we mentioned in a former chapter, are the steps by which all Hawks are trained to fly any particular quarry.

Passage Hawks are principally valued for their Heron-flying qualities; they will also kill rooks, curlews, Norfolk plovers, and even gulls*, but are of no us efor game hawking until under such command as to "wait on." Before they "wait on," they will not return to the Falconer like nestlings; it is therefore necessary to ride up to them with a live pigeon, as upon the termination of an unsuccessful flight they are

---

* Mr. Knox mentions the fact of the Peregrine Falcon, in its wild state, killing the large herring gulls. A trained bird belonging to one of the authors did the same feat: this bird (a Passage Hawk of the third year) took ducks and rooks well.

apt to start after any bird that may attract their notice at a distance.

The Heron has, at all times, been considered the most noble quarry at which the Falconer could test the qualities of his favourite birds; the height to which it will rise in the air when pursued, together with the powerful weapon of defence it carries, being such as to try to the utmost the courage and endurance of the boldest Falcons. Many Hawks, in fact, will not attack this bird at first, and can only be induced to do so by fastening pieces of meat upon the back of a captured heron and making them feed there; the bill of the heron being at the same time enclosed in pieces of elder, so as to prevent injury to the Hawk; after that, two or three herons should be given from the hand, and in a creance, before the Hawk can be depended upon to fly one at large. Herons may be caught by means of a long string, with a slip-knot, forming a noose*, which is placed round a nest, at sunset, containing eggs, and drawn over the legs of the parent bird upon her return to the heronry†. When first taken, herons refuse to feed, and must be crammed, and also have a piece of broad tape tied round the neck to prevent the food from being disgorged again. As these birds are by no means abundant anywhere, as few of them as possible should be killed.

For heron-hawking two things are absolutely necessary, viz. a well-stocked heronry, and an open country around it, easy to be ridden over. The season for this sport is during the spring months, when the old herons have to provide for their young, and for that purpose make regular flights to and fro some well-known feeding ground and their nests, often to the distance of several miles. This is called " the Passage,"

---

* This snare must be so set that the wind will not affect it and draw the noose up.

† When herons have to be conveyed anywhere, the best plan is to hood them, and carry them in a bass such as joiners use for taking their tools in.

and of it the Falconers avail themselves in order to intercept the herons upon their return.

A heron put up out of a pond or brook will not afford anything like a proper flight; for if not taken at once by the Hawks, it lights either upon a neighbouring tree, or even on the water. Probably our forefathers took in this way all the herons they used for the table, either with Eyess Falcons * or with female Goshawks. The Dutch Falconers introduced the vastly superior mode of flying this quarry by placing themselves *down wind* of the heronry, and waiting for the return of the old birds. Those which are seen going out to fish, are styled " light herons," and are not, generally, interfered with. When, however, a bird is noticed returning homewards with a full crop, the warning cry of " Au vol " is raised, and if it passes sufficiently near to the Falconer, he throws off a cast of Falcons † down wind of it, and the sport commences. Immediately the heron perceives itself to be pursued, it commences to rise in the air, or, in Falconer's language, to " ring," and at the same time lightens itself of the contents of its " creel," so that trout, eels and frogs may be

---

* During the spring of 1854 Mr. Newcome took several herons with Eyess Falcons; this being the first recorded instance of nestling Hawks taking herons upon " the Passage."

† Some Hawks are very pugnacious and intolerant of a companion: we have known Eyess Falcons compel a Sea Eagle to sit down. Wild Peregrines often attack Eyesses, and sometimes fatally. On one occasion, when Mr. Fleming (whom we have mentioned in other parts of this work) was hawking woodcocks in the neighbourhood of the Clyde, he had a flight with a young Tiercel, which brought the quarry into the river. The Hawk then made his point, and whilst waiting on, a wild Tiercel from Dumbarton Rock made a stoop at him, which brought him dead upon the water, and immediately returned to the cliff, as if highly satisfied at having slain an intruder upon his hunting-ground.

Whilst Mr. Newcome was flying his old Passage Hawk " Sultan " at a rook on Brandon Common, his bird was soon joined by a wild Falcon, which assisted in the chase; the rook escaped and the Falcons separated. Soon after this a partridge rose, and the wild Falcon caught it, but she was not allowed to " take her pleasure on it," for " Sultan " soon came up and robbed her of it.

occasionally seen entirely out of their natural element descending from the skies : the Hawks also have to get to their pitch by a spiral course*, so that the three birds may sometimes appear to be flying in different directions. The heron having considerably the start of its pursuers, is enabled to gain a lofty pitch before they can overtake it : it is this that adds so much to the interest of the scene, it being an acknowledged rule amongst Falconers, that the higher the birds rise, the finer may the flight be considered. As soon as the first Hawk has got above the heron, it makes a stoop, which is evaded by a shift; this gives the second Hawk time to take up a similar position, and in turn to make a like attempt. These stoops are repeated frequently, the birds continuing to rise, and, generally, going down wind, obliging the company to ride briskly in order to keep them within sight, often to the distance of two or three miles. At length one of the Hawks succeeds in " binding," that is, seizing the heron, its example being immediately followed by the other, when the three birds descend slowly to the ground. Instinct teaches old Falcons to unbind just before they reach the ground, in order to avoid the shock, which the young Hawks that retain their hold are liable to suffer from. Advantage should be taken by the Falconer of this unbinding to lure off the Hawk by means of a live pigeon in a creance, and to secure it, as there is great danger in attacking the heron upon the ground : it is under these circumstances, and not, as has often been supposed, whilst in the air, that he makes deadly use of his formidable bill. The Falconer, upon dismounting to secure the heron and his Hawks, pulls out a leathern thong with a leaden weight attached to it, from a bag at the side of the saddle, which prevents his horse from straying, and as soon as the Hawks have fastened upon the pigeon-lures, he seizes the heron by the

---

* A tame otter in the possession of one of the authors has been noticed to rise from deep water in the same spiral manner.

neck, and placing the bird's head between his knees, examines carefully any injuries it may have received during the encounter; if not severely hurt (which is seldom the case), or required for the training of younger Hawks, it is restored to liberty, a thin copper plate, with his name and the date of the year engraved upon it, having been previously fastened round the leg of the captive. This copper ring is secured by putting the tongue at one end of it through an opening at the other, and bending it back:—*vide* Plate XXIV. fig. 1, representing a ring, which one of the authors saw upon a heron that was taken during the spring of 1844 near Hockwold in Norfolk, by Mr. Newcome's Hawks. This heron, at the time it was taken, was on its "passage" to the Didlington Heronry *, and from the engraved date, had evidently been taken fifteen years before, near the same locality, by Colonel Wilson; showing that in all probability these birds attain a great age, and at the same time annually visit the same breeding place. This bird having been also taken the previous year by Mr. Newcome, was again released with three rings upon its legs, an honour which probably few herons would covet. The black pendant feathers at the back of a mature heron's head are (like the brush of the fox) looked upon as the Falconer's trophy, which trophy is eagerly ridden for by the members of the Loo Club, and worn, set in jewels, in the cap.

Much depends upon the wind and the quality of the Hawks, as respects the duration of a heron's flight: about the year

---

* Didlington, near Brandon, Norfolk, has long boasted of its Heronry, which, we are happy to say, is still carefully preserved. It was near this, at High Ash, that Colonel Wilson kept his Heron Hawks for many years. Latterly they became subscription Hawks, and were retained until 1836, when they were given up. These Falcons were " Passage Hawks " from Holland, and the stock was kept up by obtaining fresh birds from that country. On one occasion, soon after the breaking out of the war with France, the Falconers, who were bringing a supply of Falcons to Didlington, were taken prisoners and sent to the Hague, and subsequently to Paris.

1844 there was a wonderful Hawk at Loo called "Bulldog," which generally took her heron at the third stoop *, a feat we have never heard of as accomplished by any other Hawk.

During the spring of 1843, Mr. Newcome had a cast of Passage Hawks of such excellence, that their performances are well worth recording. These Hawks, named "Sultan" and "De Royter," had been flown for a season at Loo, before being brought to England. Each year, as soon as they had finished their moult, they were entered and flown at rooks † previous to the commencement of the heron season; during their third year they took at Hockwold in Norfolk and at Loo fifty-four herons, and in the following season of 1844 they took in the same localities fifty-seven herons!

The bittern used to be a favourite quarry at which to fly Heron-Hawks; as, however, this bird is so seldom met with at the present day, it is unnecessary to say anything about it.

Wild geese, which in some localities are found in considerable numbers during the winter months, might be taken by Falcons of the highest quality, though for this quarry the more powerful Icelander would be preferable.

In plumage the adult Peregrine differs materially from the same bird of the first year : the nestling colour, of dark brown with longitudinal markings on the breast and thighs, gives place to a rich slate colour on the upper parts of the body and wings, being darkest on the head, flight feathers and tail, and lightest on the upper tail-coverts and scapularies; the breast and thighs are at the same time barred with transverse markings of a dark grey tint, the ground colour being often white or creamy-white, particularly upon the throat and upper portion of the breast; the lower parts, including the thighs and under tail-coverts, being stained with grey.

---

* There are one or two instances of Falcons which invariably broke the wing of the heron; this is but rarely the case, and such Hawks should not be used for heron flying.

† Heron-Hawks should always be entered in the first instance at rooks.

In respect, however, to the ground colour, there is great difference in several individuals, the Falcons being usually darker than the Tiercels. Plate IV. represents a specimen of the dark variety of Falcon. We have, however, seen this reversed, viz. specimens of the female bird with a white ground, as also very dark males; they differ also frequently in the marking of the cheeks; in general the dark patch proceeding from the angle of the mouth downwards presents the appearance of a moustache, with an interval of white between it and the dark colour at the back of the head and neck; sometimes this light interval is absent *, and the bird resembles the "black-cheeked Falcon" of Australia (which may probably prove to be only a variety of our Peregrine). After the first change, there is but little alteration at the subsequent moultings; a fact which Mr. John Hancock has recorded from observation of the Iceland and Greenland birds, contrary to the previously received opinion respecting the change of plumage in these Falcons.

In studying the natural history of birds, it is interesting to observe how the laws which regulate the change of plumage from the nestling to the adult states, are modified to suit, as it were, the requirements of the different orders. Thus, the rapacious birds, whose existence depends upon their strength of wing, do not lose any of their feathers during the first year, at a time when their immatured powers of speed and endurance would be greatly weakened by the absence of any of the principal plumes. They retain the entire nestling plumage until the following spring, at which season the young of other birds offer them an abundance of food easily obtained, while at the same time they have acquired strength and skill by many months' experience. In their case, also, the period of change is extended over several months, so that but few of the principal feathers are wanting at any one time. Among

---

* An adult Tiercel marked in this manner, in our possession, is remarkably black on the back, and at the same time has a very white throat and breast.

the aquatic birds, which pass a great portion of their time on the wing in search of food, as the gulls, this process is even slower, and they appear to be longer in acquiring the adult state. The Rasorial birds, on the contrary, as also the Swimmers, change their feathers very rapidly, and when only a few months old. Many of the smaller tribes, as the finches, &c., change only the smaller feathers of the body during the first autumn, but retain the long feathers of the wings and tail until their second moult; while the summer sitants, as the swallows, make an entire change during the period of their absence from our shores; or, at any rate, do not return here until they have put on their perfect garb. Many species do not breed until they have gained the mature plumage, whereas others produce young whilst they themselves are partly clothed in their own nestling colours.

CHAPTER VI.

THE MERLIN- AND HOBBY-LARK HAWKING.

THE Merlin, in proportion to its size and strength, is perhaps the boldest of all the British Falcons, and as it is easily obtained upon the northern moors, should form a part of every Falconer's establishment; it breeds late in the season, the young birds being seldom ready to take before the end of June; the nest is formed upon the ground amongst heather, and contains in general four young ones*. The females are somewhat larger than the males, but not in the same proportion as in the case of the Peregrine. It is a remarkably tractable little Hawk, but, from its delicacy of constitution— one requiring considerable care and skill in its management— while young, the Merlin must be fed at least three times during the day; and even when in training it requires some little food in the morning, as soon as it has cast, and also must be well fed later in the day; it does not bear hunger like the larger hawks, being very subject to die from fits if not kept in good condition. It must be flown long at hack. We have kept them indeed for months in a state of almost entire liberty, by feeding them well the first thing in the morning and again during the afternoon. For use, however, this Hawk should be taken up after being at large for a month or six weeks, broken to the hood, and confined to small funnel-shaped blocks, or upon the perch (*vide* Plate VII.); or, what appears to answer still better, kept (several together) in an airy room, everything being made as

---

* Young Merlins are always infested with a large flying parasite, similar to those upon swallows or young black game ; these insects disappear soon after the young Hawks can fly.

smooth and round as possible to prevent injury to their feathers; by this treatment we have preserved several in health until the second moult.

While at hack the Merlin should be invariably fed upon the fist, and in fact always accustomed to fly there for food like the short-winged Hawks. In some respects it combines the properties of the Falcons and Hawks; like the former it has the true dentated beak and short powerful legs and feet; but in its mode of flight it somewhat approaches the style of the latter, for although it will mount to a great height in the pursuit of its quarry, still its usual mode of chasing is in a horizontal line, without requiring to rise much above its game in order to make a descending stroke. It will be found upon examination that the form of the wing indicates this modified action, being much shorter in proportion to the general length of the bird than in any other of our Falcons; and having the second and third feathers nearly of the same length, the third sometimes, if anything, having the advantage, and from that cause not so pointed in form. In activity, however, it is unequalled, except perhaps by the Hobby. Pigeons which often outfly the Peregrine, try in vain to escape this smaller enemy; and the Peregrine itself we have often seen buffeted about by our tame Merlins with impunity, although the former made many attempts to punish their impertinence *. Care must be taken not to have young Peregrines and Merlins flying " at hack " together, because the former, being nearly a month in advance of the others, would be almost certain to destroy them; as soon, however, as both species have acquired their full powers, the Merlins are safe, whilst at liberty.

The strongest female Merlins may be trained to fly pigeons admirably, and from their small size, and the way in which

---

* On one occasion two of our Tiercels gave a little male Merlin a long flight, but without being able to take it. There are instances, however, of trained Peregrines having caught Merlins.

they follow every turn and shift* of the quarry, are better adapted for this chase than the Peregrine; unlike it, they do not stop when the pigeon takes cover in a hedge or tree, but dash in and generally secure it. The first few pigeons they are flown at should be young or weak birds, so that the Hawks may not be overpowered in the struggle; and it is as well to use a cast for this quarry, though we have seen a single Merlin take even strong carriers (*vide* Plate VIII.). Their courage is such, that, in the wild state, or even whilst at hack, they may be seen driving about rooks, wood-pigeons, or in short any bird that may come in their way†.

The quarry which, however, affords the finest flight for the Merlin is the sky-lark; this is similar to Heron-hawking in miniature; the Merlin was used for this purpose by our ancestors‡. Of late years, however, Mr. Newcome appears to be the only Falconer who has tried it with success upon a large scale, which he did about the year 1850. This gentleman found that the lark proved such a severe match for his little Hawks, that he did not put bells upon them, and also that it was necessary to keep them *constantly* at larks, otherwise the Merlins gave up taking them well. When a Merlin " puts in " a lark, the Hawk should be taken down with a dead lark in a string and the live one secured; it will be found near the spot where the Hawk stopped, and so frightened as to be easily caught. A supply of live larks should be always kept

---

* We once saw a Merlin in pursuit of a swallow, which chase continued as far as the eye could trace it, the Hawk being about a yard behind its game, and following the most rapid evolutions of the swallow, as if moved by the same impulse.

† As an instance of this, we may mention a fact communicated by a friend in Northamptonshire, who had a couple of female Merlins flying at hack in 1853. On one occasion a heron passed over the house, high in the air; the two little Hawks immediately gave chase, came up with, and repeatedly struck at their gigantic quarry, to such an extent, that the heron came down nearly to the ground, uttering its loud cry of fear. One of these Merlins proved a very good pigeon-flyer.

‡ See Chaucer's " Assembly of Birds."

in an aviary for this sport, to encourage the Merlins, by throwing one up from hand, after unsuccessful attempts at the wild ones. Larks are easily kept loose in a room by feeding them with turnip-tops, bruised wheat, bread, and hemp-seed, with a supply of water. These birds are taken in numbers during the winter months by the use of the trammel-net, or during the flight season in October and November by large clap-nets, with a revolving mirror to attract them. Other small birds may be easily taken with a pair of bat-folding nets at night, and kept in a room like the larks, in which there should be a *quantity of thorn branches* for them to creep amongst, it being necessary, in order to preserve the Merlins in health, to feed them in a great measure upon their natural diet. These little Hawks require the bath frequently: in breaking them to the hood, however, they must not be drenched, as is sometimes done in the case of restless Peregrines; in fact, they are so tractable and easily managed, by quiet handling, as not to require any such treatment. Their great fault is a strong inclination to carry; to prevent this, two of them should be flown together, and as both of them will claim a share in any capture that either of them may have made, their holding on to the same bird will prevent it being carried.

Blackbirds and thrushes out of a turnip-field give very good sport, provided there is sufficient space; and even partridges may be flown with some of the best birds *, particularly such as have been accustomed to take pigeons.

The Merlin has a mode of killing its quarry, especially that of any size, as pigeons, &c., peculiar to itself, viz. by strangulation. The other Falcons despatch their prey by breaking the neck or skull immediately upon seizing it, while the short-winged Hawks kill with the foot, being provided with remarkably long and sharp talons for the purpose. The Merlin,

---

* In Ireland the Merlin is called the Snipe or Bog Hawk from its partiality to this game. Those trained to take larks might succeed with this bird also.

on the contrary, clutches its victim by the throat, and holds it thus until dead, without further injury by bill or claws, except with quite small birds, which it treats much in the same way as the other Falcons.

In plumage the *female* Merlin differs but little in the young and adult state, the old bird having merely a greyish tint mixed with the dark brown of the back, without the light edging to the feathers which distinguishes those of the first year, the breast being similar at all ages, and marked with long dark splashes on a dusky white ground (*vide* Plate VIII.); the edging of the feathers of the back, shoulders and scapularies is rusty, the shaft of each feather being distinctly lined with a darker tint of brown; the cere changes from blue to yellow, the legs and feet acquiring at the same time additional colour.

In the *male*, the change of plumage at the first moult is much more marked. The young bird, being similar to a female, loses the brown colour on the head, back, wings and tail; this is replaced by a uniform deep slate-blue with black shafts to each feather, the tail having a broad black bar near the end, with a light tip, and sometimes three or four indistinct narrower bars upon each feather. In this respect individuals differ considerably, some of them having very distinct bars on the tail, while in others there is only the broad one at the bottom. The breast and throat are white, with an imperfect ring round the neck stained with buff-red, and marked with oblong blackish-brown spots * (*vide* Plate VII.).

THE HOBBY.

This, the most elegant of all the smaller Falcons, visits our island only for the breeding season, and even then confines its wanderings within the limits of the southern and

* The albino variety of this bird has been seen; though we have never met with a preserved specimen.

midland counties. It has been rarely seen as far to the north
as the counties of Durham and Northumberland, but beyond
that range its appearance would be only accidental. It has
now become rare in England, and in consequence of the destruction of the old birds upon their arrival at their favourite
haunts, the young are but seldom to be obtained. In many
parts of Europe, however, particularly towards the east, it is
found to be common.

With greater length of wing than any other Falcon, its
high-flying qualities are considerable; unfortunately, however, it does not appear to possess the same courage which
animates its spirited little congener the Merlin; and although it was much in use in former days for the capture of
larks, it was more in combination with nets, than by its own
unaided powers of wing, that the quarry was taken. In its
wild state the lark appears to be its particular object of pursuit, and from this cause the approach of the Hobby creates
more terror among these birds than that of any other species
of Hawk; it was by taking advantage of this panic that the
sport of catching larks in a net with the assistance of the
Hobby, called " Daring," was long practised; at the present
day, however, the London bird-catchers seldom make use of
the bird for the purpose.

During the latter part of the summer and early autumn
months, the Hobby is flown over ground where larks abound;
the young of the year, and even the old birds which at that
season are going through the moult, are afraid to rise whilst
the Hawk is over head, and allow a light trammel-net to be
drawn over them by a couple of bird-catchers, by which
means great numbers of them can be taken. The sport, however, partakes more of the regular bird-catcher's than the Falconer's practice, and should only be followed by the latter for
the purpose of procuring live larks at which to fly his Hawks.
As this little Falcon is remarkably tractable, there is no difficulty in teaching it to " wait on:" what the Falconer has to

overcome in it, is a disposition to depend upon him instead of itself for food.

We can say little or nothing from experience regarding young Hobbies, as it was only in our school days that we were enabled to obtain these birds from the nest, when they were merely kept as pets. A few years ago we procured several adult wild-caught Hobbies, and endeavoured to train them for larks. We found they soon became very tame; so much so, that in six weeks from their capture they would "wait on" steadily, and return to the fist, without any further lure; they would readily fly any small bird from the hand; and it was by their "carrying" these that we eventually lost the Hawks. They did not, however, show the same readiness as the Merlin, to chase any lark or other small bird sprung from the ground, and they refused to attack pigeons altogether. We have no doubt, however, but that nestlings may be trained to fly well at bagged larks; and as they seem to be tolerably hardy in constitution, the young Falconer should not omit any opportunity he may have of testing their good or bad qualities. Those we had did not appear to suffer from the cold of the winter months, though kept entirely in the open air.

A very interesting account of the habits of this little Falcon, received lately from an officer (himself a practical Falconer) now at the seat of war, shows, that it is not in the pursuit of feathered game alone that the extraordinary powers of flight of this Hawk come into play. Our correspondent, after mentioning that these birds (of which he had shot several for examination) were very abundant in Bulgaria during the summer months, describes their habit of hawking at large dragonflies. These insects he had frequently seen them take, seizing them with the foot, and devouring them whilst in the air. He, however, at the same time, alludes to their power, as well as inclination, to kill a higher description of game, as he had witnessed the capture of the swift, lark, turtle-dove, and bee-bird by these same insect-eaters.

In olden times this was the Hawk allotted to a "young gentleman," and may be now recommended to the notice of the tyro in Falconry, as a bird very easily managed, and certain to please by its elegant appearance in the air, as well as its amazing rapidity of flight. A few months ago, the upturned eye of a Merlin on its block caused us to look in the same direction, where, at a great height, we recognized the swift-like form of the Hobby, passing with the rapidity of a messenger of ill beneath the clear sky—it was at the time on its journey southwards. Leadenhall Market is, perhaps, the most likely spot in which to meet with young Hobbies, as during the season young Hawks, as also other birds and beasts of various denominations, may be seen there; and we know of several instances in which Hobbies have been there obtained.

In plumage (*vide* Plate IX.), the young and adult birds do not vary very considerably. In the young, the upper portion of the body is nearly black, the edges of the feathers alone being of a rusty tint, while the whole of the under surface is of a dingy-white ground-colour, marked with long dark splashes. In the adult, the edging to the feathers on the back and wing-coverts disappears, the colour is at the same time changed to a dark slate, with the head, cheeks and primaries nearly black; the chin pure white in the male, dingy in the female, with a white ground-colour for the breast, marked in a similar manner to the young bird; the thighs and under tail-coverts acquire at the same time a fine clear rusty tint, the former being in the female splashed with dark spots; this is sometimes also the case in the male; more usually, however, with him, the rusty portions are without marks. The cere in the young bird is blue, which, as it increases in age, changes to yellow, and ultimately to a fine orange; the legs and feet altering in the same manner from greenish-yellow to a deep chrome. The eyes are dark hazel.

CHAPTER VII.

THE JER OR GYR FALCONS.

THE general term of Jer or Gyr Falcon of the older writers on Ornithology evidently comprehends three distinct species, inhabiting the same or neighbouring countries, and which, from the localities each particular species has selected for its breeding ground, are now recognized by the names of Iceland, Greenland, and Norway Falcons.

The two former have been, and still are by many naturalists considered merely light and dark varieties of the same bird. Mr. John Hancock of Newcastle-on-Tyne,—who, from the opportunity he has had for many years of examining great numbers of the skins of each bird, is perhaps better qualified than any other naturalist to judge correctly on the subject,— was in 1838 the first to publish the opinion he entertained of the specific distinction to be made between the Iceland or dark and the Greenland or white birds; and he considers that subsequent inquiry has only confirmed such opinion, as we find from a paper in the ' Annals of Nat. Hist.' Feb. 1854. The point of difficulty in this view of the case is, that both species are precisely alike in size and comparative proportions, which is perhaps more than can be said of any other two distinct species known, and would go far to incline us to the belief that they are merely varieties of the same bird, were it not for the universal difference of colour and markings between the young of the two species, as well as the fact that *only* the dark birds breed in Iceland, although at other seasons of the year both sorts are met with together, as well on that island as also on the American coast.

Between some of the adult birds of the two species there is

occasionally but very little perceptible difference (as may be seen from our Plates X. and XII.), either as regards colour, or the form and disposition of the markings. It may be mentioned, however, that the specimen of the adult male Iceland Falcon (Plate X.), in the possession of P. I. Selby, Esq. (from which our drawing was made), is the lightest variety of the bird we have seen; but still is darker in the ground-colour of the back and wings, which is tinged with grey, than even a dark variety of the Greenland Falcon, where the ground-colour is pure white. The usual plumage of the adult male Icelander approaches in colour to that of the female bird we have given in Plate VI.

In the light-coloured variety, here represented, it will be seen that the bars on the tail are distinctly marked on every feather; whereas, in most of the Greenland birds, the majority of the tail-feathers are either white with slight freckles, or very indistinctly barred.

The whole of the nestling Iceland birds are dark in colour; but amongst those of the Greenland species many will be found of a lighter tint than some of the adults, and all of them are lighter than any of the adult Icelanders.

There is no doubt whatever about the specific distinction of the third or Norway species, as this bird differs considerably in colour from the other two. It appears more like a link connecting these species with the Peregrine Falcon, and it seems to have much of the character of the latter bird.

THE ICELAND FALCON

is perhaps the species most usually referred to by the old writers when speaking of the Jer Falcon, and is certainly the one most easily to be procured at the present day. With steam communication between this country and Iceland, there would be no difficulty in procuring many of the young birds every

season, as they are to be purchased in the country at a moderate rate, and have only the difficulties and expense of the
voyage to overcome. Unfortunately great numbers of them are
sacrificed annually for the purpose of supplying the cabinets
of ornithologists, even to such an extent, that excellent skins
of these birds may now be purchased in this country for less
than the cost of a Peregrine. Many of these, however,
come from Greenland, whence it might not be so easy to receive them alive. These Falcons were formerly, we believe,
considered the property of the King of Denmark *, and numbers of them were yearly obtained from Iceland to be presented as royal gifts to the other courts of Europe. So great
a value was attached to these birds, that we naturally conclude that their qualities, when fairly tested, were equivalent
to it. The few, however, which of late years have been made
use of by Falconers, have not come up to this high standard.

During the autumn of 1845 Mr. Pells brought over several
of these Falcons † for the Duke of Leeds and the Loo Hawking
Club. Those kept in England were trained at Mr. Newcome's; but, from some cause or other, they did not realize
the expectations formed of them; as they failed in taking
hares, and only one or two out of the number proved good
Heron Hawks, the best being a Tiercel called "Morock."

This Falcon occasionally visits these islands during the
winter months, as does also the Greenland species. Of the
former we have seen two specimens, both young birds; but

---

* Mr. Lloyd, in his 'Scandinavian Adventures,' informs us, that in the year
1754 a ship brought 148 of these Falcons from Iceland to Copenhagen. The
same author also says, "The nests of the Norwegian Falcons were leased by the
King of Denmark to a family in Flanders;" also, that "he has seen in an old
Swedish newspaper for October 1761, a paragraph stating that some Falconers
from Ansbach in Germany passed through the town of Linkoping with 44 live
Hawks, which they had taken between Jutland and Norway."

† One of these (a male) is still alive in the Zoological Gardens, Regent's Park,
and must consequently be ten years old.

as yet we have not met with an adult Icelander killed in this kingdom.

The Iceland Falcon was formerly used in this country for flying the fork-tailed Kite*, which forty or fifty years ago was a common bird in many districts, although now so seldom seen. This sport † was much followed by the Earl of Orford and Colonel Thornton about the year 1773, and by Mr. Colquhoun of Wretham near Thetford about 1785 : Brandon Warren in Norfolk, and the neighbourhood of Alconbury Hill, in Huntingdonshire, were favourite localities for Kite hawking. Sir John Sebright relates the mode in which this sport was carried on, viz. that the great owl (*Strix bubo*), to the leg of which the Falconers attached a fox's brush, was thrown up for the purpose of drawing the kite down, upon which the Falcons were slipped at him ‡. This Falcon was also sometimes employed for taking hares. We consider, however, all ground-game quite beneath the notice of a bird possessing such power of wing as a Falcon, and would leave it entirely to the Goshawk §.

* In the time of Henry VIII. the kite was preserved in London and other towns on account of its services as a scavenger.

† An old sportsman informs us, that he can remember Kites were quite common about Gledhow—or as it is now spelt Gledhoe—near Leeds, where they built in a wooded hill. As Gled signifies a kite, and How or Hoe a hill, it is quite clear that Gledhoe, or the Kite's hill, has derived its name from being a favourite locality for this Hawk.

‡ From information we have received from travellers, it would appear that the raven is a favourite quarry of the Iceland Falcon's. This is somewhat confirmed by an anecdote which was told us by an old keeper (now dead) who had been in Colonel Thornton's service. The account was, that when the Colonel lived at Thornville Royal, he flew an Icelander at a raven which had passed over the park towards Harrowgate ; the country was then open, and the raven making down wind, was captured near Almescliffe, about nine or ten miles from Thornville Royal.

§ The Iceland Falcon in the Newcastle Museum belonged to Lord Orford, and was used by him for taking hares ; after its death he gave it to Mr. Tunstall of Whitecliff, Yorkshire, at the demise of which gentleman it was sold, and thus came to Newcastle.

At the present day Iceland Falcons that are trained to "*wait on*," might be used for grouse and black-game hawking, as also for herons, wild geese and ducks, and probably also for gulls, rooks, &c. When employed for taking hares, it was customary to use a dog also, in order to prevent the hare from squatting. The general training is the same as the Peregrine requires, and experience alone can point out the proper mode of treatment these birds may need. As they are natives of a very cold climate, they should not be exposed to the full heat of the sun. Buffon states that the Falcons carried from the north of Russia as far to the south as Persia, do not, in consequence, lose any of their powers.

The weight of a female Iceland Falcon is about $3\frac{1}{2}$ lbs.; its length from bill to tail about 23 inches, the spread of the wings being above 4 feet; the length of the male bird is about 20 inches. In colour and markings both sexes are alike, as well in the young as in adult states; individuals differing only as they assume the light or dark varieties of plumage with the intermediate gradations. The two Plates we have given of the adult male and female birds show the extremes of this difference. The tarsi are feathered about half-way down, and the naked parts are in the young birds of a blue lead-colour, as are also the cere and skin about the eyes. This colour changes to yellow in the mature birds, and deepens with age. The young birds are all of them, on the upper parts of the body, of a dark greyish-brown colour, each feather being margined with dusky white; the under surface is of the same dusky white, marked thickly with longitudinal blotches of the dark colour of the upper parts; the thighs and under tail-coverts having long streaks, which in the adult plumage are changed into transverse bars, similar to, though not so distinct as, those in the Peregrine. The colour of the irides is dark hazel*.

* We have heard of an instance in which the irides of an adult male Iceland

THE GREENLAND FALCON

This, the most beautiful of all the family, appears to be more widely distributed than its closely allied neighbour of Iceland, as it is found throughout all the northern regions of the Old and New Worlds *. It occasionally visits this island, where, from the whiteness of its plumage, it is very easily recognized. Many notices of its appearance are recorded in different works on Ornithology ; the only specimen, however, that we have actually seen is that of a young female bird in the collection of Mr. Selby, obtained by him in Sutherland-shire. A beautiful adult bird, presented by Sir J. Johnston, Bart. to the Scarborough Museum, was shot during November 1854 near Hackness in Yorkshire, which, from the description we have received of it, must be a finely marked old bird †. In olden times this Hawk was placed at the head of the most noble Falcons.

In size and proportions (as we have said before) it is similar

---

Falcon, shot at the nest, were of a reddish orange colour. The same variety has been known to occur in the Hobby and Merlin.

* We have been informed by travellers, that some few *large white Falcons,* which must be Greenland Falcons, are caught annually on their passing over the Caspian Sea, and that they are highly prized by the Falconers of Syria and Persia. We have two instances of the Greenland Falcon being kept alive in this country, and as the first was brought to London in an American ship in 1848, and was bought for the Zoological Gardens, Regent's Park, it was probably taken when exhausted at sea. The other was caught in the rigging of a ship, between Greenland and Scotland in 1841, and was brought to Edinburgh, whence it came into the possession of Mr. John Hancock of Newcastle-upon-Tyne.—*Vide* Ann. and Mag. of Nat. Hist., Feb. 1854.

† Of occasions on which this noble species of Falcon has been seen in Britain, though not obtained, we may mention, that Mr. Haywood of Lavington saw one in Wiltshire. Colonel Bonham and his Falconer, M'Culloch, on two occasions saw a large white Falcon upon the moors of Strathconnan in Ross-shire about the year 1840. In the spring of 1850, Mr. St. John and Mr. J. Hancock saw a Greenland Falcon upon Loch Spinic near Elgin.

to the Icelander, and even in colour some of the adult birds of the two species approach very closely to each other, viz. the darkest of the Greenland and the lightest specimens of the Iceland birds. The figure we have given in Plate XII. is of the average colour, some being darker, whilst others have fewer bars upon the back and wings; and some are nearly quite white, with only a few black marks on the upper parts of the body, the under portions, tail, and head, being spotless. The young birds of this species are sometimes as white as their parents, differing only from them in the colour and shape of the markings. These, as will be seen from Pl. XIII., are of a browner tone and more oblong. The legs, cere, &c. in this species are, when young, of a light bluish lead-colour, changing into yellow with age, but of a lighter tone than in the Iceland birds.

These birds, like all the Falcons, assume their perfect plumage at the *first* moult, and do not, as has been supposed, become lighter in colour each successive year. The irides are dark hazel.

THE NORWAY FALCON.

This is the third and least known of the three species we have described under the title of the Jer Falcon of the older writers. Buffon appears to have been aware of its existence, and speaks of the Norway species as distinct both from that of Iceland, as also from the white or Greenland birds *, and as being held in highest estimation by the Falconers of his day, in consequence of its possessing more courage, activity, and docility than either of the other species.

We are indebted to the kindness of Mr. John Hancock for the means of giving a figure of this noble bird (Plate XIV.).

* Both the Greenland and Iceland Falcons, particularly the latter, are occasionally to be met with in Norway.

His specimen* is a male bird of the second year, showing the change of plumage from the nestling to the adult state, and presents very much the appearance of a large Peregrine. This species might be obtained from Norway at the present day, and would probably well repay the trouble and expense of seeking.

The male bird from which our drawing was made (with the exception of the greater length of tail) was almost of the same proportions as a large female Peregrine, though with a less powerful foot; but this must have been a very small specimen, for upon the authority of several Falconers we find it is generally of the same size as the Greenland and Iceland species. The tarsi are partly feathered, similar to the other northern Falcons, and in colour also it is intermediate between the adult Peregrine and the darker varieties of the Icelander; the legs and cere in the young bird are blue lead-colour, becoming yellow when adult. This species, though possessing great power of wing, appears to be very local, and we have never heard of a specimen in any stage of plumage having been met with in these islands.

* This Falcon was originally netted in Norway by E. C. Newcome, Esq., about the month of August 1839, along with two others. They were all young birds; two were Tiercels and one was a Falcon. They were trained by Mr. Newcome, from whom Mr. Hancock received this specimen. In July 1840 or 1841 two Falconers from the Loo Hawking Club visited Norway for Hawks, and succeeded in netting nine or ten Norwegian Falcons, which were all young birds.

CHAPTER VIII.

OTHER SPECIES, FORMERLY USED IN THIS COUNTRY IN FALCONRY.

THERE are three or four additional species of Falcon always made mention of by the older writers, as being well known, and in constant use in their day; in regard to which, it is impossible to suppose that men, to whom every serviceable species of Hawk was familiar, could mistake for Peregrines of the first year, birds of which they minutely describe the distinctive marks and peculiarities. Nevertheless, for the last century, it has been the habit of writers on ornithology to deny the existence altogether of some of these disputed species, and to set down to the want of scientific observation in the old authors, the origin of several Falcons, which, as modern museums did not contain specimens of them, it was asserted were merely peculiarly-marked varieties of one well-known species. We must therefore attempt the task of vindicating the correctness of the older writers, and of showing that, at any rate, three species of Falcons are met with in Europe and the north of Africa, quite distinct from the Peregrine, which do answer to the descriptions these writers give under different names of Hawks used and valued in Falconry, and which (as they are at this day obtainable) may be again tried.

Mr. Gould, in his splendid work on the ' Birds of Europe,' gives a figure of the *Lanner*. This is one of the lost-sight-of races, and perhaps the one most frequently alluded to in old works as being in constant use. The difficulty, at the present day, is to determine *which* existing species is the true Lanner of Falconry; and we know of no other means of coming to a decision on the point, than by following as closely as possible the given descriptions of the birds.

THE SAKER.

This powerful Falcon (Plate XV.),—for the opportunity of representing which we are again indebted to Mr. John Hancock*, who kindly lent us, for the purpose, a remarkably fine specimen,—which is still to be found throughout the eastern parts of Europe, and also we believe in Asia, very closely answers to the description given by Belon of the Saker or Sacre: and as we also find in the 'Gentleman's Recreation,' a work on "Hunting, Hawking, Fowling and Fishing," of the date 1677, under the same name, a corresponding description, we may fairly conclude that these accounts were taken by the authors from birds actually before them. Belon says, that "in colour the Sacre is something like a Kite, a sort of smoky red, the dullest in plumage of all the Hawks used in Falconry, with blue legs and feet (when young); that it is a bird of passage, and was taken by the Falconers in the islands of the Levant, Cyprus, Rhodes, &c.; that it was employed for flying the Kite, but was equally serviceable for every other sort of game, and was similar to the Lanner."

From the 'Gentleman's Recreation' (page 211) we learn, that " she is somewhat larger than the Haggard faulcon; her Plume is rusty and ragged, the sear of her foot and beak like the Lanner; her pounces are short, however she hath great strength, and is hardy to all kind of fowl; she is more disposed to the field a great deal than to the brook, and delights to prey on great fowl, as the hern, the goose, &c. As for the crane, she is not so free to fly at her as the Haggard Faulcon.

---

* We have seen three or four other specimens of this bird besides that here figured, all of them in Mr. Hancock's possession. One pair of adult birds in the same brown plumage, only worn and bleached with age, was killed in Hungary in 1848 at their eyrie, which was in a tree, and came into Mr. Hancock's hands through A. H. Cochrane, Esq., who received them from the person who shot them. Mr. Hancock had also a living specimen of this species.

The Saker is good also for lesser fowl, as pheasant, partridge, &c., and is nothing so dainty of her diet as Hawks long-winged. This Hawk will make excellent sport with a Kite, who, as soon as she sees the Saker (the male whereof is called a Sakeret) cast off, immediately betakes herself to and trusts in the goodness of her wings, and getteth to her pitch, as high as possibly she may, by making many turns and wrenches in the air; which if well observed, together with the variety of contests and bickerings that are between them, it cannot but be very pleasant and delightful to the be-holder. I have known in a clear day, and little wind stir-ring, that both the Saker and Kite have soared so high that the sharpest eye could not discern them; yet hath the Saker in the encounter conquered the Kite, and I have seen her come tumbling down to the ground with a strange precipi-tancy."

This author (whoever he may be), has evidently a personal acquaintance with the bird he describes, and has also been an eye-witness to its performances.

From the size and power of the game at which it was flown, it was clearly not a young Peregrine; and the localities from which it was obtained preclude all possibility of its being one of the large northern Falcons. The bird of which we have given a figure, and which, as we previously stated, may to this day be found in the same regions, answers every de-scription of the Saker, both as to size and colour, as also in another most important point, which proves that both it and the Lanner differ from all the other European Falcons, viz. *that neither of the sexes alter the colour of their plumage* in the first and subsequent moults. This shows that they con-stitute a distinct section of the Falcon family.

The bird we have figured (which Mr. Hancock considers an adult female) is about the size of a male Iceland Falcon, having the tarsi partly feathered, similar to that bird, and with a less powerful foot, in proportion to its size, than the

Peregrine; the bill is short but very strong, and the whole formation of the bird indicates power and swiftness.

THE LANNER.

In giving a figure of the bird we suppose to be the true Lanner of Falconry, we must confess to a certain amount of distrust as to the correctness of our opinion, in consequence of not having seen several specimens from which to form a better judgment.   In all points, however, excepting the trivial one of the ground-colour of the breast, the bird we have figured corresponds exactly to the description given by the old writers of the Lanner.   Every other species of Hawks with which we are acquainted varies as to the ground-colour of the plumage in different individuals; we may suppose, therefore, that the Lanner is subject to the same rule: and that, viewing it in this light, may decide that the rufous tinge on the breast and thighs of our bird is not a sufficient cause to disqualify it from being of the species of which the breast is said to be *white*, but similarly marked.   Our bird appears to be like that from which Mr. Gould made his drawing of the Lanner.   It is, however, the only specimen we have hitherto met with; it was purchased by one of the authors some years ago from a dealer in London, who had received it (as he said) from Germany as a young Peregrine, amongst several other skins of that Falcon, and was willing to sell it as such.   It differed, however, so materially from any young Peregrine that the author had ever met with, that he was induced to try and discover of what species it really was: the result of his search led him to consider that he had found the *true Lanner* of Falconry.

For a description of the Lanner we must again refer to Belon, and the authors quoted in the 'Gentleman's Recreation.'   The former says:—"The Lanner commonly makes its eyerie in France, on the highest trees in the forest, or in the loftiest rocks. It is of less size than the Falcon-gentle, and of more elegant plumage than the Saker, especially after the moult; it is also less powerfully armed than any of the other Falcons. Any one may recognize it without any chance of mistake, because it has the beak and feet blue; the plumage in front spotted with black on a white ground, with the marks along the feathers, and not transverse, as in the Falcon."

We find a very similar description in the 'Gentleman's Recreation,' pp. 212, 213; it is this:—

" The Lanner is a Hawk common in all countries, especially in France, making her eyerie on high trees in forests, or on high cliffs near the sea-side.

" She is lesser than the Faulcon-gentle, fair plumed when an enter-mewer, and of shorter talons than any other Falcon. Those who have the largest and best-seasoned heads are the best Lanners. With the Lanner, or Lanneret, you may fly the river; and both are very good also for the land.

" They are not very choice in their food, and can better away with gross victuals than any other Hawk.

" Mew'd Lanners are hardly known from the *Soar Hawks* (and so likewise the Saker), because they do not change their plume.

" You may know the Lanners by these three tokens :—1. They are blanker Hawks than any other. 2. They have less beaks than the rest. 3. and lastly, they are less armed and pounced than other Faulcons.

" Of all Hawks there is none so fit for a young Faulconer as the Lanner, because she is not inclined to surfeits, and seldome melts grease by being over-flown.

" There are a sort of Lanners which eyerie in the Alps, having their heads white and flat aloft, large and black eyes, slender nares, short and thick beaks, and lesser than the Haggard or Faulcon-gentle. Some are indifferent large, some less, and others middle sized. Their mail is marble or russet; their breast-feathers white and full of russet spots; the points and extremities of their feathers full of white drops; their tails and train long; they are short-legged, with a foot less than that of a Faulcon, marble-seer'd; but being mew'd the seer changeth to a yellow.

"The Lanner never lieth upon the wing after she hath flown to mark, but after once stooping she maketh a Point, and then, like the Goshawk, waits the fowl.

"If she miss at the first down-fall and kill not, she will consult her advantage to her greatest ease.

"These kind of Hawks are highly prized in France and Italy, neither is she despiseable in England; but we look upon them as slothful and hard-mettled; and therefore if you intend to have any good of her, keep a strict hand over her; for she is of an ungrateful disposition, and will slight your kindnesses, contrary to the nature of the Faulcon-gentle."

It is quite certain that the bird here spoken of could not be a young Peregrine, because the very points in which it differs from that bird are particularly alluded to. That the Lanner was at one time common in France, and other countries, and yet now-a-days but seldom to be found, we can easily imagine, when we remember how birds that were quite common (as the Kite) in this country fifty years ago, are now considered rare prizes when obtained; and as also, to *the ordinary observer*, the Lanner and young Peregrine differ but little in appearance, it is quite possible that the rarer bird may have been constantly mistaken for the other. Its appearance, however, does not lead the Falconer to suppose that much would be gained, beyond settling a doubt in Natural History, by introducing it again (if procurable) to the sports of the field. A "slack mettled" Hawk is, of all others, the least likely to repay the trouble of training, and while the Peregrine is to be readily obtained, another species, almost identical in size, but inferior in power and courage, is scarcely to be wished for. The bird we have figured as a male Lanner differs from the young Peregrine in having a large rufous patch streaked with brown at the back of the head; in having the tail much more distinctly and more closely barred; in having the under tail-coverts entirely free from markings; in having the spots on the breast much more round in shape, and fewer in number; in having not so many, and those smaller, splashes on the thighs; in not having the light edging to the dark-brown feathers of the back and shoulders; in not having nearly so long or so powerful a foot and talons, and in being altogether of rather a smaller size. In our specimen the cere and legs have certainly been yellow: this would lead us to suppose that it was an adult bird. As, however, these parts change their colour and assume the adult tint *before* the commencement of the first moult, the plumage may still be that of the first year, especially as Mr. Gould, writing with specimens of both ages before him, says, "that the young of the year have the breast much more strongly marked with brown; and the whole of the upper surface of a darker tint than the adult birds." It differs from the Saker in its much smaller size, darker plumage, and in not having the tarsi partly feathered like that bird.

THE BARBARY FALCON.

This beautiful little Falcon in colour and markings is a perfect miniature likeness of the Peregrine, and might be taken for a dwarf variety of that bird, were it not for its proportional difference. It forms, in our eyes, the "beau ideal" of what a Falcon should be, and is a perfect model of strength and speed combined. For although smaller by nearly a fourth than the Peregrine, it has the organs of destruction, such as the beak, feet and talons, fully as large, united to longer and more pointed wings in proportion to its total length—in this respect almost rivaling the Hobby.

Little mention is made of this bird by the old authors; but what is said appears to apply to the species we have figured. We will now transcribe the account given of it in the 'Gentleman's Recreation,' page 208 :—

"The Barbary, or, as some call her, the Tartaret Faulcon, is a bird seldom found in any country, and is called a Passenger as well as the Haggard. They are somewhat lesser than the Tiercel-gentle, and plumed red under the wings, strong-armed, with long talons and stretchers.

"The Barbary Faulcon is venturously bold, and you may fly her with the Haggard all May and June. They are Hawks very slack in mewing at first; but when once they begin, they mew their feathers very fast.

"They are called Barbary Faulcons because they make their passage through that country and Tunis, where they are more frequently taken than in any other place, namely in the Isles of the Levant, Candy, Cyprus and Rhodes."

The specimen in our possession is that of a young male, and was killed by an acquaintance in the country from which it takes its name. Its length is under 13 inches from beak to the end of the tail; length of wing from shoulder to tip 11 inches, with the bill, legs, and feet equal in size to those of the male Peregrine. The young female is scarcely to be distinguished from the young male Peregrine except by the greater development of these organs of destruction, which equal those of the Falcon. The cere in the young bird is blue and the legs yellow, similar in this respect also to the Peregrine.

CHAPTER IX.

ON THE SHORT-WINGED HAWKS.

THE GOSHAWK.

THE Goshawk, and its miniature neighbour the Sparrow Hawk, were the only *true* " Hawks " ever used in this country in Falconry; and probably the whole of the short-winged species similarly employed elsewhere, will be found to be members of the two genera *Astur* and *Accipiter*, which these two birds individually represent. They are termed short-winged or true Hawks in contradistinction to the longer winged Falcons, from which more noble race they materially differ, both in disposition and likewise in greatly diminished powers of flight; they are also called Hawks of the fist, because it is thence, and not from a lofty pitch, that they start in pursuit of their game. From this circumstance it is absolutely necessary that the Falconer should approach very close upon the quarry before springing it, otherwise these Hawks will not even attempt to follow.

The Goshawk is, at the present day, seldom met with in England or Scotland, and can only be regarded as a rare visitant. We have seen but one specimen killed south of the Tweed. Young birds for training must, therefore, be obtained from Germany or Sweden. There is not the same necessity for flying young Goshawks "at hack" which exists (as we have elsewhere mentioned) as regards Peregrine Falcons and Merlins.

Sir John Sebright appears to have held the Goshawk in very low estimation, and expresses his surprise that any one could make use of such a bird for the purpose of *sport*. Undoubtedly, when compared with the noble Peregrine, it must take but humble rank; still the Goshawk has its admirers, and in the East is more highly prized than any other species, with one or two exceptions. In this country we find it so deficient in speed compared with that of our game, that it is evidently not so well suited to the West, since it can only be flown successfully at hares, rabbits, pheasants, and the *young* of other birds, or at coots and moorhens. It is true that much game may be *obtained* by employing it to frighten half-grown partridges, so as to enable the spaniels to catch them; this, however, can scarcely be termed *sport*, and in our estimation it would be much better to keep the bird entirely to fur hawking, in which it appears to advantage. One great point in its favour, however, is the fact that it may be used in even a thickly enclosed country, where it would be useless to attempt flying the Peregrine. The peculiar flight of the Goshawk, combined with the great elasticity of its feathers, enables it to make its way through thick cover without injury to itself. Above the eyes also there is an additional protection in the shape of a projecting cartilage, which is stronger and more prominent than that with which the Falcons are provided.

The male of this Hawk is far more active on the wing than the female; it has even been sometimes known to take strong partridges. If, combined with this degree of speed, the bird has sufficient strength to hold a full-grown rabbit, as much may be done with it as can be expected from any Goshawk. Some years ago Mr. Birch of Wretham in Norfolk had a bird of this description. In 1851 we were induced, by the encouragement and assistance of Mr. Barker, to try one of these birds. This gentleman, during a residence of many years in Syria, where the species is in great favour, was accustomed to use the Goshawk, and has taken three hares in one day with an old favourite female bird which he kept for seven years; with the same bird, also, he has taken in a couple of days as many as 42 Francolins in the *second* flight: the Francolin it must be remarked, however, is not nearly so strong upon the wing as our English partridge, nor are the hares so large. To sum up the good and bad properties of the Goshawk, we may say, that in an enclosed country, where no better species can be used, this bird is well worth the trouble of training to rabbits, or in the case of a strong female, for hare hawking, as also for flying pheasants; other points in its favour are a hardy constitution, and a readiness to thrive upon any coarse sort of food, as also the power of flying repeatedly during the whole day, with a less chance of being lost (because it does not fly far at a time) than when a Falcon is used.

On the other side, the Goshawk, however well trained, will not work at all unless in good temper and proper flying order, termed in the East "*yarak*;" but will probably take perch in a tree, where it may remain a long time, and then fly off to other trees, paying no attention to any lures, as a live rabbit or a pigeon in a string, which is of course most annoying to those whose chance of a day's amusement depends upon its will; neither will it return (like the Peregrine) to its master after an unsuccessful flight, but requires him to go in search of it: it has always the appearance of an unwilling slave, being both timid and suspicious.

Training consists in accustoming it to sit quietly upon the fist, which can only be accomplished by *constant* " carriage," and "manning" it, or accustoming it to the presence of strangers. In this respect it is to be treated exactly as we have already described when speaking of the fresh-caught Passage Hawk, with the exception of the use of the hood— the hood being never put on the Goshawk except whilst travelling. When off the fist it should be fastened to a bow-perch (*vide* Plate XX.) upon grass, or else to the Assyrian stand (*vide* Plate XXI.), the former mode, however, being the most secure. From this perch it must be taught to come to the fist for food; and as soon as it will do so readily, it should be carried out, at feeding time, secured by a creance, and accustomed to do the same from the ground, or from off a gate, and afterwards from the low boughs of a tree.

It is a good plan, also, to give the bird live mice and rats to kill amongst the grass, in order to make it eager, and easy of approach; the latter also tend to break it from the fault of carrying, which it will not do for fear of being bitten.

As the most tempting lure for a Goshawk (which is unfortunately not in "*yarak*") is a live pigeon, a Goshawk should be made acquainted with pigeons, by being allowed to kill and eat two or three thrown out to it in a string.

A stock of live rabbits must now be laid in, which are easily secured by means of nets and ferrets. Two or three of these rabbits must be given to it in a string: if it seizes and holds on, the rabbit should be killed and the bird allowed to feed on it. As soon as the Hawk can be trusted at large, and has already taken some of the rabbits in the way mentioned, it should be belled upon the tail and taken out, *sharp set*, and offered a rabbit, to the neck of which is attached, by means of a slight collar, about a yard of single string; this string is then doubled, and each string being divided in the form of a V, is tied to the ends of a light piece of cane. This splinter-bar like contrivance, to a certain extent, impedes the animal, and the strings drawing the cane straight, prevents the rabbit's escape into a hole.

It must be remembered that one great point in the successful training of all young Hawks, is to avoid, as far as possible, disappointments in their early attempts; this necessitates the sacrifice of some few unfortunate birds or beasts, which have no chance of escape given to them, but is, in reality, little more than what other sports demand, such as cub hunting with fox-hounds, and the numbers of young grouse or other game annually destroyed in the process of dog-breaking before the commencement of the shooting season.

As soon as the young Goshawk will take rabbits treated as above described, it may be considered ready for the field. Should it be, however, a strong female bird, and intended for hares, it must be first entered at rabbits, as just described, and then at leverets found in the field; it should afterwards be kept to hares *alone* if it be expected to take them well. The male birds are not powerful enough to hold a hare; in fact, it is only a few of them that will take rabbits.

Colonel Thornton was accustomed to make use of the Goshawk, along with spaniels, for taking pheasants. This the bird was trained to do, either from the perch or upon the wing; for the former mode a bagged cock pheasant in a creance was placed upon the bough of a tree, and the Hawk allowed to seize it, when both were lowered to the ground amongst the dogs. The male bird is more suited to this game than the female. In former days wild ducks were taken with this Hawk; this could only have been done by coming suddenly upon them in a brook with deep banks, as, when fairly upon the wing, these birds can easily outfly the Goshawk. Water hens and coots it can take easily, and (although we have not heard of its having been tried) it would probably be very deadly amongst young black game during the early part of the season.

When flying the female Goshawk at hares, the nearer she is brought to the seat the better will her chance be, though she may come upon them from a tree.

For taking rabbits this bird is perfect, and from eight to a dozen of these animals may be killed during the day with one Hawk. They show the best sport in a rough, rocky country, where the rabbits may be found sitting out at some distance from their holes, with the assistance of a good dog or two that will set the quarry*.

---

* Some of the finest flights at rabbits one of the authors ever had, were amongst rocks and wild juniper bushes at the seat of R. Gillow, Esq. at Leighton Hall, Lancaster.

The Goshawk is, perhaps, the most difficult of all the Hawks to manage well, in consequence of the sulkiness of its disposition, as well as its great powers of abstinence. When, however, it is in good flying order, it may be worked for a longer time than any other Hawk. It is quite useless to take the bird out except when in "*yarak*." This happy condition may be known by the erect crest, eager look, and puffed-up plumage, together with the peculiar cry of hunger. If, combined with these signs, it sits perfectly still upon the fist, moving only its head about, in watch for the expected game, there is little fear of the result. Should it, however, on the contrary, bate, draw in its feathers, and utter a chirp-like twitter, it had better be returned to its perch, for these are certain signs that it will not fly.

It requires about ten days to get this Hawk into "*yarak*;" when, however, this point has once been gained, it may be retained so for some time by judicious feeding and constant work. In order to accomplish this, the bird should be carried for an hour or two, or more, each morning, and fed only to the amount of a *quarter of a crop* upon small pieces of beef, for which it must come to the fist from the ground or perch, or it may be allowed to pull at a very tough piece while on the hand. After about a week of this drilling, should the bird manifest the proper symptoms, allow it to kill something and make a full meal; the following day it must be carried a good deal and fed very lightly, and the day after taken to the field for regular work; when in full work it should have daily from half to three-quarters of a crop, with a good gorge on Saturdays. Goshawks do not require nearly so much food as Peregrine Falcons, and will thrive upon a coarser description, rabbits and rats with a little beef being perhaps the best diet they can have. They can be moulted very well upon the low perch; and as this Hawk generally bates in one direction, a bath, made from a large earthenware cream bowl, should be sunk in the ground within reach of the leash on the side towards which it does not go when bating. In the field this Hawk will not always come readily to the fist, as, for instance, in a sulky fit upon missing its game; under these circumstances a lure of a dead rabbit or bird may be used with advantage (although it is a bad habit to indulge its obstinacy in any way). Time may be gained by throwing this lure in a string up to the bird if on a tree, and so bringing it to the ground; beef is the most attractive bait to offer this or any other hawk.

Rabbit hawking can be taken up in the spring after the game season is over, either an old pointer, or spaniels or terriers being employed for finding the quarry; with these dogs the Hawk must be well acquainted, as it is very shy of anything strange; or if a ferret* is used for bolting the rabbits from their holes, the bird must be equally well acquainted with it; if kept and fed much in each other's company this acquaintance is soon effected. Immediately upon the capture of a rabbit, the Falconer should go up and kill it, rewarding the Hawk with morsels from the head, such as the eyes, tongue, brains, &c.; this will induce the bird to seize its game by the head, which is the only secure part it can fix upon.

Goshawks do not appear to suffer from "standing" idle for a long time, as after a week or ten days' drilling they work again as well as ever. They should never be flown when at all wet, as they are almost sure under such circumstances to take perch. As they are very powerful in the foot, and when feeding are apt to use their talons rather indiscriminately, it is advisable that the hand be well protected by a strong buckskin glove, which may be cleaned with a mixture of rue and starch made to the consistency of cream.

The colour of the young Goshawk differs considerably from

---

* After the use of the ferret, rabbits are apt to desert their holes for some days, and sit out on the open ground, and in such situations afford excellent sport.

that of the mature state (*vide* Plates XVIII. and XIX.).
During the first year the whole of the under portion of the
body is of a rusty salmon colour, marked with long lanceo-
late streaks of blackish brown; while the upper part is liver-
brown, each feather being margined with reddish-white. At
first the eyes are grey; this colour gradually changes with age
to lemon-yellow, and eventually becomes orange; the cere is
wax-yellow, with the tarsi and feet of a deeper tone. At the
first change the whole of the under plumage becomes light-
grey, striped transversely with narrow bars of a dark brown
colour, the top of the head, back, wings, and tail becoming
of a uniform hair-brown, with five distinct bars of a darker
colour on the latter; there is also a streak of light grey over
each eye, speckled, as are the cheeks, with minute brown
splashes. The bars on the breast of the adult birds differ
considerably in width in different individuals : the under tail-
coverts are pure white.

CHAPTER X.

THE SPARROW HAWK.

THIS bold little Hawk so much resembles the subject of the preceding Chapter, that it might be fairly called its miniature portrait; the principal difference between the two consists in the legs and feet of the Sparrow Hawk being longer and more slender in proportion to the rest of the body; in temper also it is very similar. Its prey, however, consists entirely of birds; this Hawk being the only British species which lives solely upon its own order: all the others, more or less, make an occasional meal upon the smaller quadrupeds, reptiles, and insects. In its wild state the Sparrow Hawk is so determined in the pursuit of its quarry, that it has frequently been known to dash through a window in order to seize some cage bird *; and we have witnessed a trained one force itself to such an extent into a blackthorn bush, where it had killed a bird, as to require to be cut out.

Like the Goshawk, it is flown from the fist, or, as it is termed, "at the bolt," and starts at once into full speed, which, for a short distance, is very considerable.

The young birds are ready to be taken from the nest about the middle of June; they are very subject to the cramp if removed at too early an age. This disease affects them in a different manner to that in which it attacks the Peregrine, as it merely paralyses the lower extremities without breaking the bones; it, however, renders the birds equally useless, and is incurable.

* We have received more than one living Sparrow Hawk, captured after dashing through a pane of glass; and on one occasion we saw a male of this species chase and take a sparrow amidst the houses of a large town.

Like the Goshawk, the Sparrow Hawk does not require to be flown " at hack."

As nestling Sparrow Hawks are inclined to scramble out of their basket, and wander away *before* they can at all fly, there is considerable danger of some of them being lost in long grass, or destroyed by cats or weasels, both of which animals we have known to carry them off whilst young and helpless. Under these circumstances most Falconers prefer bringing them up in a large empty room, until they can fly well. If, however, allowed to fly " at hack " they very soon learn to prey for themselves, and should be taken up directly they begin to absent themselves at the accustomed hour * ; for this purpose we have always used the bow net. They require to be very highly fed whilst at liberty together, as the first feeling of hunger will cause the most deadly attacks upon each other, which generally end in the weaker ones becoming the food of their brothers and sisters.

When taken up, this Hawk should be treated in exactly the same manner as the Goshawk, viz. carried as much as possible, never hooded, except while travelling, and placed upon the bow perch (*vide* Plate XX.) ; it will not, however, bear the same amount of fasting, but on the contrary requires to be highly fed.

When first placed upon the fist the Sparrow Hawk displays an amazing amount of obstinacy, and will even appear to have lost all power in its legs ; so much so, as to induce any one unaccustomed to its habits, to imagine that it had received some injury. The only mode of overcoming this disposition, is to continue to replace it gently on the fist as often as it falls off, and to outdo it in resolution.

The Sparrow Hawk is mentioned by the poet Chaucer in his ' Assembly of Birds,' as being a favourite at that period

---

* Some years ago one of the authors had *nine* of these little hawks flying at hack at once, all of which came at the whistle to feed on his arm, but were at the same time very shy of strangers.

for the purpose of taking quails. As we mentioned in the 'Introduction,' the Wallachian gipsies about Bucharest, before the war with Russia, paid a tribute to the Porte in quails, which birds were taken by them in great numbers by means of Sparrow Hawks; the Hawks were caught in nets, probably whilst migrating, trained for the purpose, and again turned loose as soon as the requisite number of quails had been secured.

When landrails were more abundant in this country than they are at the present day, the Sparrow Hawk was used in capturing them, and Sir John Sebright says that it is the best of all the Hawks for this particular flight; this we can imagine, because, as the Sparrow and Goshawk do not strike down their game, but invariably clutch it, the landrail would have no opportunity of escaping by running, as it might do after having been knocked down by a Merlin or Peregrine. This Hawk can also take young partridges, pigeons, water-hens, blackbirds, thrushes, and many other of the smaller birds. It does not mount to any height like the Falcons in pursuit of its game, though it will occasionally take linnets or other birds which do mount, when it meets with them amongst cover.

Before proceeding to describe the field management of this little Hawk, we may mention the performances of some of those we have known, by way of encouraging the young Falconer. About eight or nine years ago two female Sparrow Hawks were trained by Mr. Newcome and flown at blackbirds with great success. Sir John Sebright appears to have employed them for taking partridges, and mentions having on one occasion taken a wild partridge with a Sparrow Hawk of his own training ten days after the bird had been caught in a wood. In 1851 Captain Verner (who had seen this species used by the Sikhs whilst with his regiment in India) caught 150 birds in about three months with a Sparrow Hawk of his own training. During August and part of September of 1853

Sir Charles Slingsby, Bart., took forty-seven birds with a female Sparrow Hawk. We have known the chase of a blackbird with this Hawk in an enclosed country* to last for twenty minutes; on one occasion it killed five head, viz. two blackbirds, two thrushes, and a house sparrow. In August 1854 the same gentleman took in one day eight small birds with another female Sparrow Hawk; and this Hawk killed in the space of two months nearly double the number of birds taken by the former one during the same period; but we must remark that after a time it refused taking blackbirds, and took to killing sparrows and other small birds.

In India it is the custom to *throw* the Sparrow Hawk at its quarry, by way of giving it greater impetus in the start. For this purpose it is clasped round the body by the right hand, the legs and feet of the bird being stretched behind, and so launched at the game the moment it rises, in the style of overhand bowling in cricket, without any jerk. To this process the Hawk soon becomes accustomed, and will remain perfectly quiet in the Falconer's hand. As we have said before, the directions given for training the Goshawk will apply equally well to this Hawk, small birds being substituted in the place of rabbits or hares. When made use of for flying blackbirds in an enclosed country, three or four active assistants are absolutely necessary to the sport; one of these should accompany the Falconer on the opposite side of the hedge to which he may be with the Hawk, whilst the others, by making wide circles a-head, and preventing the blackbird from escaping up the fence, must endeavour to force it out on the Falconer's side, and as near as possible to him. The Hawk is flown at the bird during its passage from one hedge to another, and if unsuccessful it takes perch in a neighbouring tree, or returns to its master's fist, or even to his head, to be ready for a fresh start; the chase lasting in this manner, on some occasions, for nearly half an hour. After each cap-

* About Knaresborough in Yorkshire.

ture the Hawk must be rewarded with a mouthful or two of the victim. Like the Goshawk, it is only when in good humour that it will exert itself at all, and this desirable state is shown by similar signs. It is worse than useless to attempt to work it excepting when it is in flying order.

It differs from its more powerful relation, however, in being of a very delicate constitution, and particularly liable to die during the first year from fits; it cannot bear hunger or cold, and should always have a few mouthfuls of food given to it early in the morning. It requires an occasional bath, and must be kept in a well-sheltered situation. The bell* should always be fastened on to the tail, as this appendage is in continual motion.

In plumage the female Sparrow Hawk, in the nestling state, differs but little from the adult bird; the principal change being, that at the first moult the feathers on the upper surface of the body lose their lighter edging, and become of one uniform brown. The colour of the breast differs very much in different individuals; even in the same nest, one or two of the young birds may have the ground-colour white, with dark brown transverse narrow bars (*vide* Plate XXI.), whilst the others may be entirely of a rusty colour, with uneven markings of a darker tint.

The *young* male bird resembles the female, but after the first year the brown colour of the back and shoulders is changed to a dark slate blue, whilst the breast is finely barred with rusty brown upon a light ground, the under tail-coverts being pure white.

Whilst very young the irides are of a greenish-grey; this colour changes with age to a lemon yellow, and eventually becomes of a bright orange tint. The cere is of a greenish-yellow, and the legs and feet gamboge, with very black claws.

---

* The bells as well as jesses used for these little Hawks should be of the lightest description: for the latter, thin seal-skin leather prepared in alum is very suitable.

Before closing our observations on the management of the different Hawks whilst in training, a few hints as to their treatment during a journey may prove of service. The safest mode of conveying Hawks is to carry the bird or birds upon the arm; this plan should always be adopted where there are not more than two of them; when, however, the Falconer has to carry about with him a larger establishment, the " spring box cadge " (as described in a former Chapter) should be used; the Hawks, being hooded, are fastened to it, as on the cadge, with their breasts turned outwards. The bottom of the box should be covered with a layer an inch or two in depth of sawdust, to absorb the moisture. The Falconer, during the journey, requires to be always in close attendance upon his birds, in case of any entanglement from bating; upon his arrival at the termination of the day's journey, if at a country inn, there will be little difficulty in finding some quiet garden where there is a plot of grass or a paddock, where the Hawks may remain unhooded until the journey has to be renewed; they are here to be fastened to the iron pins (with which, of course, the Falconer is provided) thrust into the ground, and a large smooth round stone, or inverted flower-pot, placed close to the pin, makes, for the time, a very good substitute for the regular block. Goshawks and Sparrow Hawks had better be fastened to their own bow perches, which being portable, can be carried about with the birds. When, however, he has to stop in a town, or where such a quiet spot cannot be obtained, the Hawks had better be placed unhooded on stones or flower-pots, in a loose box covered with straw. If the place is too small to peg them down, it should be rendered *perfectly* dark, as without light the Hawks will not move, and consequently cannot get at and injure each other.

It is a point of importance that none of the birds should receive any castings the day before a journey, as, if they are moved about without having previously cast, sickness may be produced. In the case of the larger Hawks, also, which bear fasting for many hours without injury, it is better not to feed them before starting. Merlins and Sparrow Hawks, however, require food in the morning, and must also be fed up well at the end of their journey.

When it is necessary to send a Hawk to some distance without any attendant, the best mode is to place it hooded in a basket sufficiently large to prevent it from being cramped, and well lined inside with soft matting. Should the long feathers of the wing or tail get bent upon the journey, they may, in general, be perfectly restored by merely dipping them in hot water. Those feathers, however, which have been previously imped, are apt to get broken, and must in that case be remended above the former join.

Hawks, before they are sent upon a journey of doubtful length, should be got into good condition, as being then far better able to endure cold or any unexpected delay they may be subjected to. However, in these days of rapid and cheap travelling, there is no excuse for running any risk with a *good Hawk,* for which it is always worth while to engage the care of a trustworthy person.

When travelling with Hawks, and the dogs intended to be employed with them in the field, it is of great consequence thoroughly to accustom the birds to the presence of their four-footed companions ; and to this end the latter should be chained up within sight of, and near to the blocks of the Hawks. A very convenient portable dog-box has been invented and used constantly for the purpose by one of the authors, and which may be called the "camp dog-box." It is made of light wood, in the shape, when put together, of an inverted V, with the addition of a base or floor of wood ; the two sides or roof are hinged together at the edge, forming the apex of the triangle. The lower edge of one of them is also permanently fastened to the floor by hinges, whilst the other is kept in its place (when in use) by means of two hooks with eyes fixed into the floor. The ends of the box are closed in

with pieces of canvass, through one of which there is a hole sufficiently large to admit the dog.   The whole, when unhooked,
can be folded together, and forms a very portable kennel, the
use of which has the additional advantage of preventing the
dogs from becoming infested with the vermin they are apt to
meet with in old stables on the road.

CHAPTER XI.

IMPING AND COPING, WITH THE DISEASES OF HAWKS, AND THEIR TREATMENT.

THE primary object of the young Falconer should be, of course, to keep his birds in perfect health and feather. As, however, both the one and the other are naturally liable to become injured, we will endeavour to describe the best modes by which he can remedy the defect.

In the case of the plumage. The feathers most liable to injury are the three first primaries of the wing, and all belonging to the tail. When one of these is broken sufficiently high up to admit of the insertion of a needle, the only thing necessary will be to cut through the feather at the broken part, and reunite it by means of an imping needle, for a figure of which *vide* Plate XXII. fig. 4. These needles are made of different sizes, according to the thickness of the feather for which they may be required. For the wing-feather of a Peregrine the needle should be about one inch and a quarter long, made three-sided throughout, gradually tapering from the centre towards each point. These needles are easily formed, by the aid of a small file, out of pieces of unannealed iron wire, cut to the requisite length; or very good ones may be made from glover's needles, which are always triangularly pointed. These should be heated in a candle to soften them a little, and then filed up on the eye side, so as to form a second point.

When, however, the feather of the bird is broken *off*, it must be restored from the corresponding one of a similar Hawk; and for this purpose the Falconer should take every opportunity of obtaining the wings and tails of any dead

Hawks he may meet with, as well as of laying by the long feathers which his own birds cast.

This process of mending a feather is called imping, and in order to do it neatly cut the broken feather with a sharp knife in a sloping direction, about its centre, with so much of the new feather as will exactly replace the part lost, at a corresponding angle; dip the needle in strong brine, or smear it with a little heated cobbler's wax, or with the patent liquid glue, and force each end of it equally far into the centre of the pith of the two portions of feather (*vide* Plate XXII. fig. 5), so as to bring them close together; this, when nicely done, leaves a join scarcely perceptible. When the feather is broken off so near to the quill that the pith of it is not solid, the best plan is to cut away the whole of the stem of the broken feather, leaving merely the quill in the body of the bird; into this quill fit one end of a small piece of light wood, used like an imping needle, by thrusting its other sharpened end into the hollow part of the new feather; this may be made quite secure by smearing it with liquid glue, and by a turn or two of fine wire or waxed silk outside. This mode will even make a less perceptible union than the former one: it should never be done, however, where the needle will succeed, as in case of a second breakage there is no way of replacing it*. Another method is to insert the shaft of a feather instead of a wooden plug, and to run the imping needle into it.

Feathers that are only bent can be restored by merely dipping them in hot water. The tail-feathers of a Hawk may be generally imped whilst the bird is sitting hooded on an assistant's fist. When, however, those of the wing have to be repaired, it is absolutely necessary that the bird should be

---

* In no case should the broken feather of a Hawk be *pulled out*, because when such is done it is seldom replaced; and even if a new feather does appear, it is almost certain to be a *crimped* and deformed one.

held. This is done as we have previously described in Chapter I.

Coping is a term applied to the shortening the beak or talons of a Hawk. This is best accomplished with a pair of sharp wire cutters, the cut surface being afterwards scraped over with a knife or fine file. It is always done to fresh-caught wild Hawks, to prevent injury from their weapons, and is also frequently necessary with trained birds, as far at least as the beak is concerned, which must not be allowed to grow too long, or it will be very liable to split and break off, or prevent the bird from feeding easily*.

DISEASES OF HAWKS.

Moulting, though it cannot strictly be termed a disease, is nevertheless a periodical return of a far greater tendency to weakness than the bird is subject to at any other season, and may as such be placed at the head of what are, more strictly speaking, maladies arising either from natural causes, or the result of accident or inattention.

The time for the commencement of the moult with Eyess Falcons of the *previous year*, when kept in good condition, is from the middle of March until the early part of April †, but when older they begin the moult later. The feather first

---

* In the wild state Hawks do this for themselves, by rubbing down their beaks upon rocks.

† By referring to notes kept for some years by one of the authors, respecting the daily management of his Hawks, we find that the 9th of April 1847 was the day, in two instances, on which the first feather was cast; and that these birds, by being kept in a warm loft, had gained their perfect new plumage, and were again in training by the 1st of October. In 1849 an Eyess Falcon was put up on the 8th of March, and was flown again, after completing the change, on the 3rd of October. In 1850 a Passage Hawk was not put up until the 18th of May, which was perfectly moulted by December 4th. The same Falcon, on the following year, cast the first feather on the 17th of April, having been previously kept in high condition.

cast is the seventh in the wing; after this the secondaries are renewed one at a time. The shoulders and breast then begin to change, and eventually the tail and primaries. The last feather cast is the first of the primaries.

Falconers adopt different modes of keeping their Hawks during this period of moult. Some wish to retain them in work; and, for this purpose, treat them as usual, and only take care that they should be in as high condition as is practicable with having them in flying order, affording them at the same time some additional shelter in bad weather. This mode, where the Hawks are used for taking herons or rooks, is almost necessary, as it is at the period of the commencement of the moult, and afterwards, that the best sport may be obtained; the drawback to the system is, that the Hawks are many weeks longer in gaining their new dress, than is the case when they are kept warm, quiet, and in high condition; and also, that the partly-grown young feathers have a greater chance of being struck out. Another plan is to keep them at rest on their blocks during the time, and to feed them up very highly; in this way they attain very perfect plumage, but lose to a certain extent in power of wing in consequence of the long period of inactivity. A third mode, and that recommended by the old writers on Falconry, is to place the birds at large in an airy chamber, each Hawk having a room to itself, the floor of which is to be covered with sand or gravel to the depth of a couple of inches, the Hawks to be at the same time highly fed, and to have a bath standing at all times in the chamber. A fourth mode, adopted by one of the authors for several years, was to place the birds, either singly, or two or three of the same sex together, in a warm good-sized loft, which, from being roofed with slate, became, during the summer months, very close and warm (having only one open and grated window to it), the floor of it being covered with sand, with the beams matted over, and a bath always at hand. In this loft, the birds having plenty of space for exercise, and being very highly fed, were found, when first flown after the completion of the moult, to be almost as active on the wing as they had been previous to their confinement, and were invariably in perfect health and feather, not any of the nestling plumage remaining, as is generally found to be the case when they are treated according to the first-described methods; and in addition to this the owner was able to resume work with them many weeks sooner than is ordinarily the case; the heat of the loft tending in a great degree to assist the throwing off of the old plumage, without in any way injuring the health of the Hawks, or rendering them more tender afterwards.

So few Peregrines are killed in this country in the transition state of plumage from the eyess to the adult feathering, that it appears as if their wanderings led them to a hot climate in which to pass their first period of moult, particularly as the autumn migration of the young birds is towards the south, and those which return to us in the spring are found to be in the adult plumage, showing that their first change of moult is passed elsewhere.

Passage Hawks, which are obliged to be kept in lower condition than nestlings, do not begin to lose their feathers at so early a date, and are longer in gaining the fresh ones. As these are the birds usually employed for heron and rook Hawking, this delay at the commencement is rather an advantage than otherwise. In order to render the growth of the feathers broad and strong, it is necessary to feed Hawks very highly during the moult. They must not be kept entirely upon beef, which would prove too stimulating. As Hawks also like a variety and require castings, they should be fed occasionally upon warm pigeons, rooks, rabbits, &c. Sir John Sebright highly recommends the yelk of a raw egg to be added to the beef, which is previously cut into small pieces. Some Hawks certainly like egg, nor is it unnatural when we reflect that every female bird which a Hawk kills in the spring is full of eggs, which we have frequently seen them deliberately pick out and eat with the greatest relish.

Hawks that have been kept in idleness during the period of the moult, and are consequently very fat at the end of it, require considerable care and management to bring them into flying condition again; it will not by any means do to endeavour to starve them at once into proper trim. The plan to be adopted is this :—as soon as the first of the primaries (which are the feathers last cast) have become hard penned (and not before this), the Hawk should be taken out of the chamber or loft, furnished with fresh jesses, bell, &c., and treated for a few days very much in the same manner as if under its first training,—probably it will now require quite as much trouble as in the first instance to make it stand well to the hood; it should be carried as much as possible for exercise, and the quantity of its food reduced not at once, but at intervals of alternate days, with a full gorge every four or five days: on the day following the gorge, little or no food need be given, and in this way it is brought down to the proper flying condition before it is trusted again at large.

The first time on which it is flown it should be very "sharp-set," flown to the lure, and well rewarded for obedience.

Before attempting to describe the various diseases by which the lives of Hawks in training are in most instances shortened, as well as the few antidotes with which we are acquainted, it may be as well to mention the age to which particular birds have been kept.

Mr. John Pells, sen., when Falconer to the Duke of St. Albans, had a Passage Falcon named "Duchess," a bird of extraordinary qualities for high mounting, speed, and certainty of stoop. At the age of eight years this Hawk escaped by breaking loose from her block at Highgate, and having been captured at the Zoological Gardens (Regent's Park), her owner not being known, she was retained there in confinement for eight years longer, making her at least sixteen years old when she died. This is the greatest age we have known a Hawk attain in captivity.

We have, however, met with several trained Peregrines which reached the ages of five, seven, eight and ten years. When not over-fed, Goshawks would probably live as long; of these we have known two or three reach eight years. With the exception of a male Iceland Falcon now in the Zoological Gardens, which is ten years old, not any of the Iceland, Greenland *, and Norwegian Falcons which have of late years been kept alive in this country have lived more than four or five years. Merlins are difficult to retain beyond the first season, though we have had some which reached the period of the second moult.

The characteristic marks of a well-made Falcon are breadth of body, particularly across the shoulders, muscular and large thighs and feet, smallness of head, with very full eyes and open nares, together with long rakish wings. The health of the bird is indicated by a brilliant eye, facility of respiration, as well as the whiteness of the mutes, the breath at the same time not being offensive. The opposite signs show that something is wrong.

THE CRAMP (*Tetanus*)

is the most fatal of all the diseases to which young Hawks are subject. Of this we have spoken under the head of treatment of nestlings; and as there is no cure for the attack, it will be useless to refer to the subject further.

---

* Of the Greenland Falcons here referred to, one was in the possession of **Mr. John Hancock**, and the other was in the collection of the Zoological Society.

The next complaint which occasionally attacks young Peregrines is very similar in its progress, and the appearances it presents after death, to human consumption. This is probably brought on by cold and neglect, and may perhaps be relieved at a very early stage by warmth, good feeding, and exercise.

APOPLEXY

is a complaint which very seldom attacks the Peregrine. Goshawks, when fat are more liable to it.

It unfortunately proves fatal to nine-tenths of the Merlins and Sparrow Hawks trained every season. Though not curable, it may be prevented or rather postponed to a certain extent by care and good management. It sometimes is caused by the bird being too fat, and when in this state, placed under a hot sun, or even by being frightened by dogs or other causes, and often occurs whilst the Hawk is bating from the fist. Merlins, which are kept as much as possible at hack or in a large airy room or case, seem to be more free from this complaint than those which are confined to the block.

EPILEPSY.

We have seen cases of this complaint amongst Peregrines, Goshawks, Sparrow Hawks and Merlins. These convulsive fits are not necessarily fatal, as the Hawk may live for weeks after experiencing the attack; probably to allow the bird to fly at hack would be the most likely mode of restoring it to health.

THE KECKS OR CROAKS

derives its name from a peculiar sound the bird makes whilst under any exertion, such as bating or flying; it seems to be a disease of the air passages, analogous to a cough in beasts; it is peculiar to the Peregrine, and attacks Passage Hawks as well as nestlings. It generally makes its appearance in the autumn and spring during the prevalence of cold wet weather, particularly where the bird has been much exposed. This, though a common, is not a dangerous disease when attention is paid to its first appearance; rest, warmth and good diet, with occasionally six or eight bruised peppercorns* given with the castings, being all that is necessary to render the bird sound again. If put up to moult in a warm loft with this disease upon it, the Hawk will probably be found to come out again perfectly free.

THE FROUNCE

is a disease of the mucous membrane of the mouth, gullet, and intestines (similar to a complaint young children are subject to, viz. aphtha or thrush), and arises also from damp and cold; it shows itself in the first instance by the difficulty in eating the bird exhibits, and it will be found that this arises from the swollen state of the tongue; upon examination, the tongue and palate are seen to be covered with a brownish white coating. When taken at an early stage, this complaint does not prove obstinate under proper treatment; if, however, it is neglected and allowed to run on without any remedy being applied, it passes downwards to the intestines, and will then very probably terminate fatally. The mode of treating it with success is to cut a quill into the shape of a pen without the split, and with this to scrape off the thickened skin from the tongue and roof of the mouth, until the parts bleed (the bird, of course, being securely held by an assistant), and after that to dress the raw surface with a little burnt alum

---

* When a laxative is necessary, a little pounded sugar-candy rubbed into the meat acts as such. Two or three grains of powdered rhubarb is more powerful, and has a very marked effect as a stomachic. It must be given when the Hawk is fasting and has had no castings. Water, given by dipping a few pieces of meat in it, acts in a similar way upon the bowels.

mixed with either vinegar, lemon juice, or citric acid, doing it freely, so that some of the mixture may pass a little way down the throat; the Hawk being fed for some time upon a light nourishing diet, such as birds, rabbits, or mice, with little or no beef, and kept warm. This dressing should be repeated two or three times a week, and should the case prove a bad one, a weak solution of nitrate of silver in the place of the alum mixture may be used.

CORNS.

Falcons are subject to small tumours upon their feet and toes, as also to a general swelling of the joints. These tumours are generally called corns, though in reality they are small indurated cysts, the contents of which may be easily removed by merely cutting down upon them with a sharp knife, and squeezing the matter out. This will succeed when little swellings are along the toes: if, however, the ball and joint of the foot become swollen, the cure is more difficult. The best remedy perhaps is what ought to have been employed as a preventative, viz. placing the bird at once upon a padded block, as we believe the evil almost * always arises in consequence of the hardness of the block or perch on which the Hawk has been kept. We, in one instance of bad swollen feet in a Sparrow Hawk, tried tincture of iodine as an absorbent, apparently with advantage. Where, however, it is the practice to keep the Hawks upon soft blocks, this disease is unknown.

THE BLAIN.

This serious complaint, which consists of watery vesicles within the second joint of the wing, is supposed to be peculiar

---

* We have seen an instance of this disease in a Falcon at liberty, which might have arisen from the bite of a crow.

to Passage Hawks; it is very difficult to cure, and one which, if of long standing, will generally produce a stiff joint, or even further disease of the bone. We have attempted to remove it by occasionally lancing the swollen part, and allowing the fluid to escape, the bird at the same time being kept as quiet as possible. Nestlings are subject the first year to a somewhat similar malady, which attacks the roots of the primaries just at the time when the feathers are attaining their full growth, and often causes these feathers to break off, leaving the stumps in the pinion. If the Hawk is good in other respects*, and can fly tolerably well under the loss of a feather or two, it will be well worth keeping until the following year, when the feathers at the first moult may come again, provided the stumps have not previously been forcibly extracted.

FRACTURES

are either simple or compound—simple, where the bone alone is broken, without laceration of the flesh, compound where the broken ends are forced through the surrounding muscles, —when either occurs to the thigh or leg of a Hawk, it may be reduced, and the bird become as sound as ever.

Nature's restorative powers in the lower animals are far greater than in man, and the most formidable-looking injuries in them may with a little care be overcome. If, however, the shoulder or wing be the parts injured, it will be found very difficult to effect such a cure as to render the bird again useful for the chase. The shoulder, in particular, is liable to form a false joint and the wing continue powerless; and even where only the smaller pinion bones are broken, the long muscles which direct them are almost certain, by their contraction, to produce an overlapping of the fractured edges,

---

* "Verbæa," an Eyess Falcon of 1853, belonging to Mr. Newcome, lost a feather from each wing in consequence of this disease, notwithstanding she proved one of the best and swiftest Hawks that gentleman ever possessed.

which soon reunite, and render the point permanently shorter, and in this way diminish its power. These injuries may occur to trained Hawks in consequence of their flying against wire fences, or from a shot or trap when "at hack" or otherwise at large.

Where the bone is simply fractured, it will be necessary to have the bird held firmly by an assistant, and after the careful adjustment of the broken surfaces, to secure the bone in its proper position either by a bandage of calico previously dipped in strong starch, which hardens in drying, or by forming a neat splint of gutta percha to fit the limb; this is easily done by softening a strip of the material, about the thickness of ordinary shoe-leather, in warm water, and while in that state moulding it to the limb, and when cold and hard, trimming and rounding the edges and sewing on tape strings. This form of splint will keep the broken parts immoveable, and after about three weeks' time may be removed, when the limb will be found straight and sound again: the plumage acts as a soft wadding between the splint and skin, and thus prevents the latter from becoming chafed. When, however, the fracture is a compound one, and the flesh much lacerated, the part should be bathed repeatedly with warm water, and not bound up tightly until the inflammation and swelling have in a measure subsided; after which it must be treated as in the former instance. The wounded bird should be kept as quiet as possible in a darkened room, and fed twice a day upon a light diet, such as the flesh of rabbits cut into small pieces and given from the hand.

PARASITES.

There are three different parasitical insects found upon Hawks, and which sometimes prove exceedingly troublesome to them. The first is a species of flying tick, similar to those seen upon swallows, young black game, and some few other birds. These insects appear to devote their attentions entirely to young Merlins. Upon these little Hawks, and these alone, are they invariably found during a few weeks after the birds leave the nest; they quit them, however, as soon as the Hawks begin to bathe, and probably attach themselves to them in the first instance more for warmth and shelter than for the sake of the juices of the feathers. They are undoubtedly derived from the ground on which this Hawk breeds, and as they so soon desert the birds naturally, there is little use in attempting to destroy them.

The second are more common and more disgusting insects, viz. lice, which may be found on all the different species of Hawks, Passage Hawks and Hobbies being however more subject to them than others. They are very easily got rid of by a strong decoction of tobacco with water, to which, after straining, should be added an equal quantity of brandy or other spirit. With this mixture the head, neck, and shoulders of the bird must be dressed by means of a good-sized camel's-hair brush. One dressing will in general prove sufficient; if, however, necessary, it may be done as often as is requisite. Some writers recommend that the smoke of tobacco should also be blown through the feathers: regular bathing tends more than anything else to keep Hawks free from these pests *.

The third insect which we shall now speak of is far more injurious to the health of the birds than the others, and at the same time is not so easily noticed: it is a species of *Acarus*, and makes its first appearance in the nares of the Hawk, burrowing in these parts, as also into the eyelids; and if not destroyed in time, its numbers increase with wonderful rapidity, eventually covering the whole body of the bird. Merlins appear to be more subject to these insects in the first instance than Falcons;

* Rooks are often infested with lice, and Hawks that are flown at rooks are véry frequently troubled by these insects, which leave the rook for the Hawk whilst the latter is killing and eating its victim.

if, however, they are not extirpated, all the Hawks kept near to each other will soon be affected. At the first appearance of any soreness about the nares of a Hawk, the parts must be well washed out with a fine camel's-hair pencil dipped in the before-described tobacco mixture, which should be thrust well into them, and examined to see if any minute dark red mites are perceptible; if so, daily attention is requisite, the nares and eyelids of the bird being frequently washed and a small quantity of the red precipitate of mercury ointment applied; the bird so affected must be at the same time removed from any others, until all appearance of the evil has vanished.

GLOSSARY

OF

TERMS USED IN FALCONRY.

ARMS.—The legs of a Hawk from the thigh to the foot.

BATE.—To flutter off the fist, block, &c.

BEAM FEATHERS.—The long feathers of a Hawk's wings.

BEWITS.—Strips of leather by which the bells are fastened to the legs.

BIND.—To fasten on the quarry whilst in the air.

BLOCK.—The conical piece of wood on which Falcons are placed.

BOLT.—To fly straight from the fist at game, as Goshawks and Sparrow Hawks do.

BRAIL.—A thong of soft leather in which there is a slit, for securing the wings of Hawks.

BRANCHER.—A young Hawk that has lately left the nest.

CADGE.—The wooden frame on which Hawks are carried to the field.

CADGER.—The person who carries the cadge.

CALLING OFF.—Luring a Hawk from an assistant at a distance for exercise.

CARRY.—For the Hawk to fly away with the quarry.

CAST.—A pair of Hawks.

CASTINGS.—Feathers, fur, or tow given with the meat to a Hawk to cleanse the gorge.

CERE.—The naked wax-like skin above the beak.

CHECK.—To fly at; to change the bird in pursuit.

CLUTCHING.—Taking the quarry in the feet, as Goshawks and Sparrow Hawks always do, also Falcons occasionally.

COME, TO.—To begin obeying the Falconer.

COPING.—Shortening the bill and talons of a Hawk.

CREANCE.—A long string.

CRINES.—The small hair-like feathers about the cere.

DECK FEATHERS.—The two centre feathers of the tail.

ENDEW.—Is when the Hawk digests her meat.

ENTER.—To fly the Hawk at quarry for the first time.

EYESS.—A nestling Hawk.

EYRIE.—The breeding place.

FALCON.—The female Peregrine and Goshawk " par excellence ; " also the general term for the long-winged Hawks.

FLAGS.—The feathers next to the principals in the Hawk's wing.

FROUNCE.—A disease in the mouth and throat of a Hawk.

FUR.—To fly at ; to fly at hares and rabbits.

GET IN.—To go up to the Hawk after it has killed.

GORGE.—The crop, or first stomach.

GORGE, TO.—To satiate with food.

HACK.—To fly at ; the state of liberty in which young Hawks are kept for some weeks before training.

HACK BELLS.—Large heavy bells put on to young Hawks to prevent them from preying for themselves whilst at liberty.

HAGGARD.—A wild caught Hawk.

HANG ON.—A term used sometimes instead of WAIT ON.

HOOD.—The leathern cap used for the purpose of blindfolding Hawks.

IMPING.—Mending a broken feather.

INKE.—The neck from the head to the body of the quarry.

INTERMEWED.—When a Hawk is moulted in confinement.

JACK.—The male Merlin.

JERKIN.—The male of the Jer Falcon.

JESSES.—Leathern straps fastened to the legs of Hawks by which they are held.

LEASH.—The leathern thong by which the Hawk is tied up.

LURE.—The instrument by which Hawks are attracted to the Falconer.

MAIL.—The breast-feathers of a Hawk.

MAKE HAWKS.—Old staunch Hawks employed in teaching the young ones.

MAN A HAWK.—To teach it to endure the company of strangers.

MEW.—To moult; also the place in which Hawks are kept.

MUSKET.—The male Sparrow Hawk.

MUTES.—The droppings of a Hawk.

NARES.—The nostrils of a Hawk.

PANNEL.—The lower bowel in a Hawk.

PASSAGE.—The flight of Herons to and from the Heronry during the breeding season.

PASSAGE HAWKS.—Another term for HAGGARDS taken upon the passage or migration.

PELT.—The dead body of any bird the Hawk has killed.

PETTY SINGLES.—The toes of a Hawk.

PITCH.—The height to which a Hawk rises in the air.

PLUME.—To fly at; to fly at birds.

POINT, TO MAKE ITS.—The mode a Hawk has of rising in the air to mark the place where the quarry has " PUT IN."

POUNCES.—The claws of a Hawk.

PRINCIPALS.—The two longest feathers in the wing of a Hawk.

PULL THROUGH THE HOOD.—To eat through the aperture in the front of the hood.

PUT IN.—Is when the quarry is driven to cover.

QUARRY.—The game flown at.

RAKE.—To fly too wide.

RAKING.—Striking the game in the air.

RAMAGE.—Wild, difficult to be reclaimed.

RANGLE.—The small stones which Falconers formerly gave their birds to improve their digestion.

RECLAIM.—To make a Hawk gentle and familiar.

RED HAWK.—A Peregrine of the first year.

ROBIN.—The male Hobby.

RUFF.—To strike the game without seizing it.

SAILS.—The wings of a Hawk.

SERVING A HAWK.—Assisting to put out the quarry from a hedge, bush, &c.

SHARP SET.—Very hungry.

SOAR HAWK.—Any Hawk of the first year.

STANDING.—Remaining in idleness at the block.

STOOP OR SWOOP.—The rapid descent of a Falcon from a height on to its prey.

SUMMED.—When the plumage is fully grown.

SWIVEL.—Used to prevent the jesses and leash becoming twisted.

TAKE THE AIR.—To mount aloft.

TIERCEL.—The male Peregrine or Goshawk.

TIRING.—The leg or pinion of a fowl (from which the flesh has been cut), at which the Hawk in training may pick at the little that remains.

TRAIN.—The tail of a Hawk.

TRUSS.—To clutch the quarry in the air.

VARVELS.—Small rings of silver fastened to the end of the jesses, on which the owner's name, &c. used to be engraved.

WAIT ON.—The Hawk to soar in circles above the head of the Falconer in expectation of the game to be sprung.

WEATHER.—To place the Hawk unhooded in the open air.

YARAK.—An Eastern term to signify when the short-winged Hawks are in hunting condition.

INDEX.

———